THE WORLD OF
BALLET

Kate Castle

KINGFISHER

KINGFISHER

Kingfisher Publications Plc
New Penderel House,
283–288 High Holborn,
London WC1V 7HZ

www.kingfisherpub.com

First published by Kingfisher Publications Plc 2005

10 9 8 7 6 5 4 3 2 1

1TR/0904/TIMS/PICA/128MA

Copyright
© Kingfisher
Publications
Plc 2005

A CIP catalogue record for this book is
available from the British Library.

ISBN 0 7534 1072 9

Printed in China

Editor: Camilla Hallinan
Designers: Terry Woodley, Steve Leaning,
    Robert Perry
Cover designer: Malcolm Parchment
Picture research: Elaine Willis, Alex Goldberg

First published as *The Best-Ever Book of Ballet*

CONTENTS

A note to the reader
The small pictures at the start of every section tell the story of The Sleeping Beauty, a ballet in four parts – a curtain appears at the beginning and end of each part. You can read the story on pages 44–45.

THE STORY OF DANCE

All over the world people dance. Dance has always been at the centre of important events such as marriage, the birth and naming of a child and the burial of the dead. There are dances for sowing crops, gathering harvests and making rain. Dance, songs and the rhythmic sounds of drums and other instruments form rituals that draw people closer together.

NORTH AMERICA
1 Buffalo dance
2 Cheerleader
3 Square dance
4 Chinese New Year dragon dance
5 Tap dance

SOUTH AMERICA
6 Amazon tribal dance
7 Latin American ballroom
8 Devil dance, Bolivia
9 Samba, Rio

EUROPE
10 Morris dancers, UK
11 Flamenco, Spain
12 Scottish dancing
13 Irish dancing
14 Wedding dance, Turkey

AFRICA
15 Egyptian stick dance
16 Masked funeral dance, Dogon tribe
17 Tutsi dancers
18 Gambian dancers
19 Zulu war dance

ASIA
20 Mongolian 'wrestlers' (dancer and puppet)
21 Khon dance drama, Thailand

All kinds of dance

Dance that belongs to a particular country is called folk dance. It is part of everyday life as well as celebrations and ceremonies.

Dance that is purely for pleasure and takes place at parties, clubs or ballrooms is called social dance.

Performance dance takes place on stage, film or television for others to watch. It uses a mixture of dance, music and design to tell a story or create a mood. There are many styles of performance dance – contemporary, jazz, tap and ballet.

► Basilio and Kitri are the principal characters in Don Quixote, a ballet set in Spain. Kitri dances en pointe, on the tips of her toes, but the ballet steps are performed in a style borrowed from Spanish folk dance. The term "ballet" comes from the Italian word "ballo", meaning dance.

Ballet is different from other ways of dancing because it uses turn-out, in which the leg is turned in the hip so that the feet point sideways, and pointe-work, in which ballerinas use specially stiffened shoes to stand on the very tips of their toes. Both turn-out and pointe-work make certain movements, such as turns, easier to do and more spectacular to watch.

22 Kathak dance, India
23 Indian classical
24 Malay rice dance
25 Court dance, Java
26 Harvest dance, Japan
27 Bugaku, Japan
28 Kandy dancer, Sri Lanka
29 Temple dancer, Bali
OCEANIA
30 Aborigional spear dance, Australia
31 All-Black haka, based on Maori war dance, New Zealand
32 Cook Islander
33 Hula dance, Hawaii

5

The beginning of ballet

Ballet began in the European courts of the 16th and 17th centuries. The court of Louis XIV of France was based at the splendid Palace of Versailles, just outside Paris. Courtiers took part in elaborate celebrations staged in gardens and ballrooms, called ballets de cour. These often had parades of horses, processions, speeches and songs as well as dance.

▼ The courtly rules of behaviour gave ballet much of its elegance and precision.

▼ Louis XIV danced in his first ballet when he was thirteen. His most famous role was as the sun god Apollo in Le Ballet Royal de la Nuit in 1653. The ballet lasted over 12 hours!

The ancient Greeks and Romans danced for pleasure, as illustrated by this frieze. Many of the early ballets were based on Greek and Roman legends.

A ballet called The Loves of Mars and Venus (the Roman gods of war and love), was performed in London in 1717. It was one of the first ballets to tell a story without using speech and song.

▲ **Frieze with a dancing bacchante, 425 BC**

W hen ballet began to be performed in theatres, at first as part of opera, professional dancers took the place of courtiers. In 1672, Louis XIV founded the Académie Royale de Danse. Its director, Pierre Beauchamp, recorded the steps and positions, including the five positions of the feet, which form the basis of today's technique.

Stars on the stage

Marie Camargo (1710–1770) shortened her skirt so that she could dance more difficult steps and show off her footwork.

Salvatore Vigano (1769–1821) and his wife, Maria Medina, wanted to bring more natural, expressive movements into ballet. They wore costumes based on those of ancient Greece.

Gaetano Vestris and his son Auguste were Italians who danced in France to huge acclaim in the 18th and 19th centuries. Gaetano was known as 'the god of dance', but Auguste also astonished audiences with his virtuoso jumps and turns.

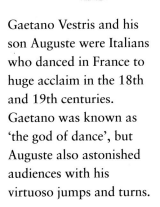

Ballet develops

By the 1830s, the costume for the ballerina looked as it does today in Romantic ballets like La Sylphide. The ballerina wore a long tutu with a fitted bodice and soft net skirts ending below the knee. Her hair was parted in the middle, draped over the ears and drawn into a low bun. Early in the 20th century, ballerinas began wearing the classical tutu, with short fluffy skirts of many layers which enhanced the steps, as they became more daring.

En pointe

Marie Taglioni (1804–1884) was one of the first ballerinas to stand on the tips of her toes, en pointe, to look as if she was floating. Ballet shoes in those days were soft, so her feet must have hurt at first. Her father, who was also her teacher, invented exercises to strengthen her legs and feet.

Romantic ballet

Romantic ballet was a reaction against all that was going on in the world. The introduction of factories and machines during the Industrial Revolution made choreographers want to write ballets that were light, airy and unreal.

Romantic ballets were about fairies and spirits and humans rising above the world. Women were seen as delicate creatures who need protecting and lifting gently.

La Sylphide is one of the oldest Romantic ballets, and it is still danced today. It tells the story of a young Scot called James who falls in love with a sylph. You can read their story on page 46.

Classical ballet

Ballerinas' steps are more daring and difficult in Classical ballet than in Romantic ballet.

In Act III of the Classical ballet Swan Lake, Odile tries to persuade Prince Siegfried that she is Odette, the Swan Princess he has fallen in love with. Odile wears a black tutu, whereas Odette wears white.

Rite of Spring

Nijinsky made a ballet about a primitive human sacrifice which shocked audiences at its first performance in Paris in 1913. With its harsh theme, it became a turning point in both ballet and music.

Since then, many choreographers have used Stravinsky's dramatic music to create their own Rite of Spring. The costumes in this production by Kenneth MacMillan allow the dancers total freedom of movement.

Late in the 19th century, choreographer Marius Petipa devised a series of Classical ballets – grand and elaborate story ballets with lavish scenery and costumes. The stories are told through set patterns, made up of solos for one person, pas de deux for two people, and small and large groups of dancers in the corps de ballet.

Modern ballets don't always have a story. Instead they can be about moods and feelings.

Modern ballet

The dancers create dramatic pictures in Apollo, a ballet by George Balanchine. Their costumes are more fitted, to show the shapes the dancers make. Apollo was a Greek god, and the three women represent mime, dance and poetry. This type of ballet, modern but with classical steps, is sometimes called neo-classical.

The dancer

Dancers are special people. They are intelligent, musical and adaptable. They have the confidence to dance solos but still work as part of a team. They use imagination to create different characters on stage. They take criticism without making a fuss, knowing that they will never stop learning and perfecting their technique. Lastly, all dancers enjoy challenges, pushing themselves and their technique to new limits by working with many different choreographers.

A star is born

Anna Pavlova was born in St Petersburg, Russia, in 1881. She was a frail, premature baby and her mother was a poor widow. When she was eight, Anna's mother took her to see The Sleeping Beauty at the Maryinsky Theatre for a Christmas treat.

Anna knew immediately that she wanted to be a dancer and two years later joined the ballet school in Theatre Street. With the help of teachers such as Enrico Cecchetti she worked hard, grew strong and was accepted for the Maryinsky company.

▶ Mikhail Fokine created the Dying Swan solo for Anna Pavlova for a charity performance in Russia. When she was dying of pneumonia in 1931, she is said to have whispered, "Prepare my Swan costume." The day after Anna Pavlova died, the cello music by Saint-Saens was played while the spotlight moved over the empty stage.

Next stop the world

Anna Pavlova had a special love for dancing that made her stand out from the rest. She wanted as many people as possible to enjoy her dancing – so for 15 years she danced all over the world, for rich people and poor, in large towns and small, travelling over 185,000km and giving over 4,000 performances. She is remembered by all who saw her.

▶ Mikhail Baryshnikov, in Frederick Ashton's Rhapsody. Baryshnikov was born in 1948 and studied at the Kirov Ballet School. He moved to the West in 1976, and danced first with The Royal Ballet. One of the great virtuoso dancers of our century, he enjoyed working in film and with new choreographers. He directed American Ballet Theatre in the 1980s, and now directs his own modern dance company, White Oak Dance Project.

◀ Another great ballerina, Margot Fonteyn, later described Pavlova as "a genius".

When dancers stop dancing, usually in their mid-thirties, they must take up a new career. Many become teachers, choreographers and directors. Others stay close to their ballet company by becoming administrators, notators and physiotherapists. The discipline of ballet prepares dancers well for completely different careers.

"I desire that my message of beauty and joy and life shall be taken up and carried on after me. I hope that when Anna Pavlova is forgotten, the memory of her dancing will live with the people. If I have achieved even that little for my art, I am content." (Pavlova)

11

▼ This class started with exercises at the barre, and has now moved to the centre of the studio to continue without the barre.

LEARNING TO DANCE

You can enjoy ballet without wanting to become a professional dancer. Ballet will give you confidence, poise and an approach to learning that will be useful in all sorts of other areas. It is important to have the right attitude to your lessons – to look, listen and keep trying even if it seems hard at first. Most important of all, ballet lessons should be fun – something you, your teacher and your audience can all enjoy.

1 The teacher gives encouragement and corrections to the pupils.

2 The pianist plays music.

3 If the pianist is away, the teacher uses tapes.

4 The ends of your shoe ribbons must always be tucked in neatly.

5 The class is doing a port de bras exercise.

6 Pupils hold the barre to steady themselves during barre exercises.

7 Mirrors help the pupils to check their positions and alignments.

8 The teacher has certificates showing she has passed examinations and is qualified to teach.

9 A rosin box, filled with a powder that stops feet slipping on the floor.

10 One pupil is practising a different exercise while the others watch the class.

11 This pupil is holding her head in the correct position. Can you spot why the others are incorrect?

12 A colourful poster reminds the pupils what they are aiming for.

◄ The painter and sculptor Edgar Degas enjoyed watching dancers at the Paris Opéra ballet in the late 19th century. This bronze figure is called La Petite Danseuse (The Little Dancer). She is 14 years old, and is standing in fourth position. Is her posture correct? (Turn to page 17 to find out.)

When you begin to learn ballet, you need to find a school with a qualified teacher. Letters after their name show that they have taken exams in how to teach and have studied anatomy, so that they understand how the growing human body works. They may teach slightly different techniques, such as the Royal Academy of Dancing (RAD) or the Cecchetti method. Some schools offer the chance to take examinations, so you can check your progress. As well as ballet, most schools have classes in other styles such as modern, jazz and tap.

► Class ends with a révérence, a bow that says "thank you" to the teacher and the pianist and is preparation for acknowledging the applause of an audience.

What to wear

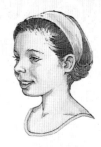

For your first lesson you can usually dance barefoot, in something loose and comfortable. After that, most schools prefer you to wear their own uniform, called practice clothes. Practice clothes fit as closely as possible so that the teacher can see clearly and correct any mistakes. Everyone tries to be as neat and well groomed as possible.

Hair

The ballet hairstyle shows as much of the face as possible and makes the head look sleek and in proportion to the rest of the body. Long hair can be pinned into a bun, or plaited and pinned on top of the head. A short style can be kept tidy with a headband. Dancing would be much harder with hair tangling in your face.

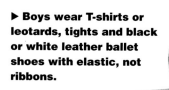

▶ **Boys wear T-shirts or leotards, tights and black or white leather ballet shoes with elastic, not ribbons.**

Getting ready

Use a bag to carry your practice clothes to class. Wash them each time they are worn, and repair any shoe ribbons that may have come unstitched. Tuck shoes inside each other to keep their shape between classes.

Legwarmers and cross-overs are usually worn only at the beginning of class, tutus at performances, and jewellery never!

Shoe ribbons

Each ribbon is about 2.5cm wide and 50cm long. Fold the heel of the shoe forward. Sew a ribbon on each side, just in front of the fold. Sew onto the canvas, not through the drawstring.

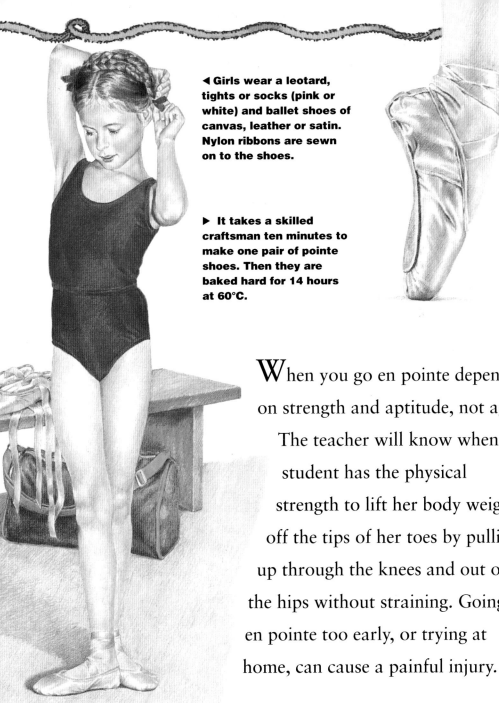

◀ **Girls wear a leotard, tights or socks (pink or white) and ballet shoes of canvas, leather or satin. Nylon ribbons are sewn on to the shoes.**

▶ **It takes a skilled craftsman ten minutes to make one pair of pointe shoes. Then they are baked hard for 14 hours at 60°C.**

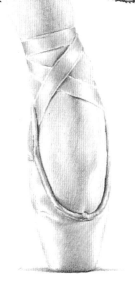

When you go en pointe depends on strength and aptitude, not age. The teacher will know when a student has the physical strength to lift her body weight off the tips of her toes by pulling up through the knees and out of the hips without straining. Going en pointe too early, or trying at home, can cause a painful injury.

Pointe shoes

In a ballet company each dancer will have her own supply of pointe shoes, stored for her either at the theatre or in large baskets when on tour. She will use about ten pairs a month, although principal dancers may use twenty!

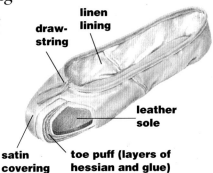

draw-string

linen lining

leather sole

satin covering

toe puff (layers of hessian and glue)

1 Keep your foot flat on the floor and start with the inside ribbon.

2 Take the ribbon over the foot, round the ankle and to the back again.

3 Cross the other ribbon over the first one: over the foot, round the ankle.

4 Tie a knot on the inside of your ankle and tuck in the ends neatly.

At the barre

All ballet classes begin at the barre, then move to the centre for more difficult steps. The barre acts as a support for exercises which warm up the muscles and prepare for the steps which come later. Much of the time at the barre is spent working on turn-out and developing good placement, or placing. This is the relationship of one part of your body to another – for example, shoulders to hips. The teacher will correct any mistakes, and you can use the mirror to help check your positions.

Hands and feet

Hands are held with the fingers softly grouped together and the thumb tucked in. For an arabesque, the fingers can be flatter and more stretched (see page 18).

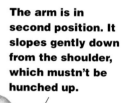

Feet point straight, as if through the middle toe. Toes musn't be clenched. A foot which curves inward is called a sickle foot.

Eyes look straight ahead. Head is level, with the feeling of a long neck.

The arm is in second position. It slopes gently down from the shoulder, which mustn't be hunched up.

This is the working leg. The leg is stretched and the knee is straight.

The arm is in third position (RAD) or fifth en avant (Cecchetti method). The dancer is finishing the plié.

Turn-out is from the hip, but the hips should stay flat to the front, not twisted or lifted so that one is higher than the other.

Knees bend and point to the side. If this hurts or is hard to do, then your feet are turned out too far.

This is the supporting leg.

1 The first exercise is to bend the knees in a plié. This is a demi or half plié in second position. Pliés improve turn-out and gently stretch the muscles.

Feet turn out, heels stay flat on the floor. They lift in a full or grand plié only in first, third, fourth and fifth positions.

2 In battements tendues, the foot slides along the floor to a point. This strengthens the feet and legs, ready for neat and fast footwork later.

Posture

Pull your seat under and stomach up so your back is straight. Keep your head straight and your chin level. Feel that your neck is long and graceful and your shoulders are in a natural and comfortable position.

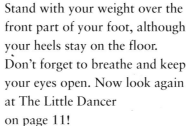

Stand with your weight over the front part of your foot, although your heels stay on the floor. Don't forget to breathe and keep your eyes open. Now look again at The Little Dancer on page 11!

Hard work and strain mustn't show in a dancer's face.

Knee faces the side, thigh well turned out.

Foot is flexed and gently rests on the ankle of the supporting leg, before striking the floor.

Foot stays flat on the floor. If your ankle rolls inwards, then your other leg has been lifted too high.

4 Grands battements strengthen the legs and improve turn-out and extension – the height the legs can be raised.

Leg is stretched, knee straight, foot pointed. Lift as high as it will go without raising your hip too much out of line.

Positions of the feet

Most ballet steps begin and end in one of the five positions of the feet. There are also five positions of the arms.

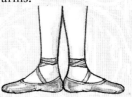
First position

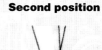
Second position

Third position

Fourth position

Fifth position

When you start ballet, barre exercises take about 15 minutes, but professional dancers are at the barre for about half an hour.

3 In battements frappés, the ball of the foot strikes the floor sharply. In double battements frappés, the heel first crosses behind the ankle and back again. This helps with jumping and beating steps.

Exercises at the barre are practised first on one leg and then on the other, turning round in between so that each side of the body grows equally strong. Most exercises are done to the front, the side, the back and the side again, known as en croix – in the shape of a cross.

Centre work

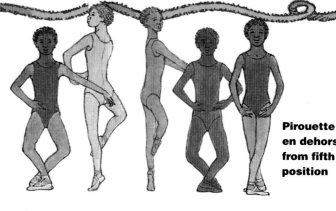

After the barre, some of the exercises are repeated without the support of the barre to improve strength, suppleness and stamina. They begin with ports de bras for graceful arms, and adage, slow sustained movements for poise and balance. This is followed by pirouettes, or turns, then petit allegro with batterie, quick small jumps in which the legs beat together. Lastly comes grand allegro, travelling and jumping steps which feel like real dancing.

Turns

A pirouette is a plié followed by a combined rise onto demi-pointe and spin. Pirouettes can turn away from the supporting leg, en dehors, or towards, en dedans. You can also turn in other positions such as in arabesque.

In an arabesque (one of the most basic and lovely poses in ballet) one leg stretches up behind the dancer.

Dancers avoid becoming giddy by 'spotting' – looking at a fixed spot at eye level for as long as possible, then whipping the head round quickly to find the spot again.

▼ First arabesque

The teacher

Ballet teachers have always been important. Some have developed the technique, others have helped famous dancers reach their full potential. Although your teacher may criticize you at times, he or she is there to help you dance your very best. Even world-famous principals do class every day and make mistakes – but they never give up!

From 1906 to 1908, Anna Pavlova was Enrico Cecchetti's only pupil.

Adage

Draw an imaginary line with your finger from the dancer's extended hand to the tip of her toe, and another from the top of her head down to her supporting foot. Practising adage helps to shape these positions.

Petit Allegro

This is a changement, which means 'changing'. Start in fifth position, jump and change the feet once, landing in fifth position with the other foot in front. You can change the feet in the air up to three times, which is called an entrechat six (3x2 legs). Wayne Sleep has performed an amazing entrechat douze (6x2 legs).

Changement

When you are learning ballet, the exercises and steps may be much the same every week, especially if you are preparing for an exam. In a professional class, the teacher will set different enchaînements, or series of steps, to test the dancers' skill and memory. This also prepares them for working with a variety of choreographers.

Petit Allegro

Pas de chat means 'step of the cat'. One leg leads and the other follows as you jump sideways, swiftly and lightly like a cat. In the middle of this step, both legs are off the ground, pointed toes meeting in the air.

Pas de chat

▲ **For a grand jeté, which means 'big jump', both arms and legs are fully stretched – you should be able to trace three curves.**

This is an exhilarating leap from The Fountain of Bakhchisarai, a Russian ballet first performed by the Kirov Ballet.

Grand Allegro

Temps de poisson means 'fish step' and looks as if a salmon is jumping out of the water in a silvery curve. Trace the shape with your finger and follow it with your eyes. The height of the jump is called its elevation.

▶ **A temps de poisson performed by Prince Siegfried in Swan Lake Act III**

19

Pas de deux

Pas de deux or double work is usually taught in a separate class. It consists of pirouettes, adage and a huge variety of lifts performed with a partner. In Classical ballets such as The Sleeping Beauty, pas de deux follow a set pattern: supported adage, male solo and then female solo, usually ending with a faster finale called a coda. The man's role is to lift the woman and support her through a series of adage steps and turns. In later ballets, the choreography is more flowing and the lifts more acrobatic.

Supported arabesque

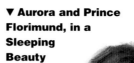

A ballerina can stand longer en pointe in arabesque with a partner's support. If the partner walks around her, while she keeps her balance, this is called a promenade.

▼ Aurora and Prince Florimund, in a Sleeping Beauty pas de deux

Perfect partners

The audience appreciates the line of the pas de deux, both dancers making curves that balance or contrast with each other in intriguing shapes. Above all, pas de deux should look effortless.

Great partnerships

Two dancers may build a strong relationship, each improving the other's performance. Great partnerships include Margot Fonteyn and Rudolf Nureyev, Suzanne Farrell and Peter Martins, Antoinette Sibley and Anthony Dowell.

Finger fouettés

The male dancer lightly holds the ballerina's middle finger above her head while she turns. She begins to turn by pushing off from the palm of her other hand in his.

Practising pas de deux means learning to trust your partner. Partners should be well-matched in size, as standing en pointe makes the ballerina much taller. Coaching in pas de deux is usually given by former principal dancers, who make sure the choreography is danced in the correct style. Pas de deux from the Romantic period are soft and flowing, while Classical pas de deux are known for elegance, clean line and greater virtuosity.

Straight lift

The male dancer lifts the ballerina over his head with straight arms. She can do very little to help him, apart from jumping at the beginning of the lift, so this position needs great strength.

◄ Full of daring lifts, the Russian ballet Spartacus tells the story of a revolt led by a Roman slave.

Travelling lift

As the woman jumps, her partner lifts and carries her across the stage, in a graceful position which she sometimes changes in mid-air. As he supports her, she must keep the line of the jump.

▼ In Voluntaries, a modern ballet by Glen Tetley, experienced dancers can experiment with more daring and difficult lifts.

Getting stronger

Male dancers build strength in arms, shoulders, knees and back by weight lifting and muscle-building exercises at ballet school, which must be properly taught to avoid injury. But boys should also remain streamlined for speed and agility. Too much bulk will spoil a dancer's line.

Sarah is eleven. She joined the ballet school at the time when most children move from primary to secondary school. Before that she had been to weekly ballet classes with a local teacher. Competition to enter the school is fierce. Sarah had to audition by dancing in a class taught by a teacher from the school, then doctors checked that her body was suitable for training. She will stay at the school until she has taken her GCSEs, when she will move on to the senior school for further training.

A day at ballet school

Sarah's day

This has been the very best day since I came to the ballet school. It took me a while to settle in when I first started six weeks ago. It was so strange to be living away from home and all my friends and family. But it's great to be with people who really understand how much I love dancing and don't get bored when I keep talking about it!

Miss Farmer's class

The day began, as usual, with an enormous breakfast at eight o'clock – no dieting here – we need to eat lots of healthy food to help our bones grow strong. We had our daily class from nine to ten-thirty and Miss Farmer said that my pas de chats were very untidy – my fifth positions looked more like thirds. But I did a perfect double pirouette, so that made me feel better. My friends stayed behind after class and we helped each other to practise. The girls have daily ballet class together, but the boys will join us tomorrow for an hour of character dancing. We are learning some of the Mazurka steps from Act I of Coppélia. We have school lessons as well, just like any other school, and I like maths, music and French. It really helps to know that pas de chat means cat's step, for example, and that glisser means to slide.

first, a big breakfast!

After lunch we had more schoolwork, and later in the afternoon, at four, we had an hour's pointe-work class, where we are learning how to rise onto pointe holding on to the barre. While we did this, the boys practised lifting weights to help them build their muscles for pas de deux. My partner is called William. He's thirteen, the same age as my brother, and he likes the same sorts of things – rock bands, football, computer games.

character dancing

Supper was at six and then, when we'd all done our homework and sewn the ribbons on our new shoes, the Principal told us that the company have chosen some students to be in the new production of The Nutcracker. The school is linked to the company, so we are sometimes allowed to watch rehearsals or take part in the productions. I am to be a mouse in Act I! Even better, I am also to be the understudy for Clara, who has a solo and dances with the Nutcracker Prince. The first night is at the beginning of December, so we only have six weeks in which to practise. I can't wait until tomorrow when a teacher from the company comes to teach us the steps! The last two weeks of November we'll spend some time with the company, rehearsing first in the studio and then on stage. Scary!

sewing ribbons

Natalie is sixteen. She will be in the Senior School for two or three years, at the end of which she might be chosen for the company. The company staff will have watched Natalie closely throughout her training. Of the twenty-five girls in her class, probably only five will be picked for the company attached to the school. The rest will audition for other companies in Europe and abroad.

Natalie's Day

I sometimes wish I were still at the Lower School, instead of living in this flat where no-one but me ever seems to do the washing-up. Life at the Upper School is very hard work. The day's schedule is crammed full and then we have to shop, cook and wash our own clothes – a bit like being in the company and away on tour.

I'm late!

Anya and I were late for nine o'clock class this morning as we forgot to set the alarm. The teacher was a guest from the company and he wasn't very pleased with us. Then we had pas de deux for an hour and began learning how to do fish dives. This was quite funny as several of us ended up on the floor. Jamie, my partner, kept making me laugh but we did it really well in the end.

After lunch we had a make-up class and then at the end of the day we had repertoire for another hour. The girls are learning corps de ballet work – the Snowflakes Waltz from The Nutcracker – while the boys are learning Colas's solo from La Fille mal Gardée – the one with all the difficult turns. When we know The Nutcracker really well, we shall be able to watch the company rehearsals. Then, if someone is ill or injured we might go on stage in their place. Everyone hopes they will get into the company, but so few actually do.

our first fish dive

Although I like the older ballets, I enjoy the newer ones too. We had workshops at the lower school on how to make ballets, and I decided then that I would like to be a choreographer.

make-up class

I am making a new piece for a studio performance and Jamie, Laura and I worked on it all evening. I can see all the steps in my imagination, and it's so frustrating when they can't get it right. They keep asking what it's about, but it doesn't have a story as such. I've just called it Two's Company. The music helps a lot. A music student has written it specially, and it's very loud with electronic synthesizers and strange effects.

After the rehearsal, Laura and I walked home. As it was after nine, we picked up a huge pizza on the way. Must remember to set the alarm!

early to bed, early to rise

rehearsing

Teamwork

While the dancers practise in the rehearsal studio, hundreds of other people are busy in costume and scenery workshops, in the orchestra pit and in the theatre offices. It is this complex teamwork that finally brings a ballet to the stage.

1 The Director runs the company. He is watching a final studio rehearsal of a new production of Swan Lake.
2 The choreographer has made some alterations to the original choreography. He checks to see if the group position is correct.
3 The notator records the choreography using symbols like music notation.

4 The accompanist plays the piano version of the full orchestral score.
5 The conductor watches some of the final rehearsals so he knows the tempo – how fast or slow the music must be played.
6 The ballet mistress, a former dancer, is in charge of the corps de ballet and helps the dancers keep in line.
7 The ballet master takes some rehearsals

and produces a schedule of rehearsals.
8 The understudies, known as "covers", watch and learn. There are several sets of dancers, or casts, for each ballet, and they take turns in performing.
9 A soloist practises an attitude at the barre. She is cast as one of the Big Swans in Act II.
10 Von Rothbart, Swan Lake's villain, waits to make his entrance.

11 A dancer fixes her shoe. As a coryphée or junior soloist, she performs the Dance of the Little Swans with three others.
12 The corps de ballet must all keep in line in exactly the same position.
13 The répétiteur is a former principal dancer who now coaches principals.

14 The principal female dancer, also called a prima ballerina, dances in the two roles of Odette and Odile.
15 The principal male dancer, a premier danseur, is Prince Siegfried. He is a guest artist from another company.

CREATING A BALLET

Ballet is a combination of dancing, music, scenery, costumes and lighting. So a new ballet is the result of a close partnership between lots of people. First there is the choreographer, who has the idea for the ballet and devises the steps. He works closely with the composer, who writes the music or creates a sound design. Then there are the designers of scenery, costumes and lighting, who decide how the ballet will look on stage. Even old classics, such as Swan Lake, can have new scenery and costumes.

▲ Edgar Degas' The Dancing Class shows that ballerinas used to rehearse in tutus, not in the kind of practice clothes dancers wear now.

The composer and choreographer

Many things give choreographers ideas for ballets – myths, legends, poetry, plays, even the Bible. These ideas are expressed in movement shaped by music. Sometimes the choreographer commissions new music from a composer. He outlines his ideas, and the composer responds with music that the choreographer can work with. Modern ballet music may use electro-acoustic instruments and unusual sounds to create its effect.

Pyotr Ilyich Tchaikovsky (1840–1893)

A composer

Tchaikovsky wrote lyrical and dramatic music for the Imperial Russian Ballet, including such masterpieces as Swan Lake, The Sleeping Beauty and The Nutcracker. Choreographer Marius Petipa would give Tchaikovsky detailed notes, counting out the numbers of bars of music he needed for each mime or series of steps.

A choreographer

Marius Petipa studied first with his father and then with Auguste Vestris at the Paris Opéra Ballet. He became Ballet Master in St Petersburg in 1869. His best-loved ballets include Swan Lake, The Sleeeping Beauty and The Nutcracker. They are known for their complex corps de ballet scenes and for their spectacular divertissements with demanding virtuoso steps.

Marius Petipa (1818–1910)

Orchestral score and dance notation for Swan Lake

Sometimes a choreographer will have heard existing music, which she feels is just right for ballet. By listening to it frequently, she begins to see stage pictures taking shape in her imagination. The company notator works alongside the choreographer, writing down the steps.

Serge Diaghilev brought composers and choreographers together to make new ballets which delighted and shocked audiences. His company, the Ballets Russes de Serge Diaghilev, performed from 1909 to 1929 and changed ballet from old-fashioned romance and fairy tales to modern emotions and vivid colour.

Top of head		
Shoulders		
Waist		
Knees		
Floor		

▲ **This is the Benesh notation for a grand jeté from La Bayadère,** Petipa's ballet about a young Indian warrior's love for a temple dancer.

Notation is a way of writing down the steps of a ballet. Labanotation is widely used in the USA and can record any movement, not just dance.

This is an example of the other system, Benesh notation. Dancers also use video to help them learn and remember the steps.

▼ **Diaghilev watches a rehearsal of Le Tricorne (The Three Cornered Hat),** a ballet set in Spain about a miller and his wife.

Choreographer Léonide Massine works with Tamara Karsavina, one of the greatest ballerinas of the Ballets Russes, and Leon Woizikowsky, a virtuoso dancer. Composer Manuel de Falla is at the piano, and the artist Pablo Picasso has brought his designs. They all loved the beauty and mystery of Spain: Massine learnt flamenco dancing to enrich the choreography.

The Designer

Besides being able to use colour, texture and perspective in an imaginative way, a designer also has to be an architect and an engineer. Some sets have balconies, windows and staircases, while others use machinery to move scenery. Sets must also be easy for the stage crew to change between acts and, in a touring production, load into trucks. Most importantly, the stage and lighting design must help the audience to enter another world as it watches the ballet.

▲ A Paris Opéra design for Act II, Swan Lake, by Bouchène

1 The designer

The designer talks to the choreographer as soon as a new ballet is planned. He or she then draws detailed pictures of each scene of the ballet.

2 The model

The drawings are made up into scale models of each scene, with miniature furniture.

▼ Model for Act III, Swan Lake

◀ Backcloth for Acts II and IV, Swan Lake

3 The backcloth

Backcloths are painted either flat on the floor, or hung vertically in a work-shop. The scenic artists work to a grid, drawn first onto the design and then onto the unpainted cloth.

The lighting designer brings even more atmosphere to the production, using coloured lights, spotlights and special effects. His lighting designs will be entered as a computer programme operated at each performance by a technician seated in a control room at the back of the theatre's auditorium.

4 The scenery

The designer keeps a close eye on the workshops as the set is being built. Skilled carpenters make the scenery, including the flats that stand at the side of the stage. They begin work many weeks ahead of the first performance.

5 The lights

The lights themselves are called a rig, and have to be set in place before each performance. They are fixed on booms at the side, or hung from a bar above the stage. At a technical rehearsal, once the scenery is in place, the lighting effects for each scene are created – the designer directs the rehearsal from a lighting desk in the auditorium.

A technician changes a gel, a coloured but transparent slide that alters the colour of a white lamp. The lamp's shutters are adjusted to alter the amount of light.

Props

Props are properties, objects the dancers will use in their hands on stage. They are made in the company's workshops. Props can be made of wood, cloth, papier-mâché or acrylic resin. They are often much lighter than they look but need to be very hard-wearing as each new ballet can last for many years.

La Fille mal Gardée: Alain's umbrella and bouquet

Cinderella: broomstick

Swan Lake: goblet

Romeo and Juliet: sword

The Nutcracker: nutcracker doll

The Sleeping Beauty: spindle

Costume and make-up

The costume designer is responsible for clothes, hats, shoes, wigs, jewellery and often make-up too. A full-length ballet may need up to 300 costumes. The designer draws and colours a separate sketch for each one, and writes suggestions for materials and trimmings such as lace, sequins or beads on the design. Sometimes samples of fabric are stapled to the design before it goes to the workshops.

Which fabric?

Fabric looks different on stage, under lights, than in daylight, and the people who make the costumes know what materials give the best effect. Dyeing gives fabric exactly the right colour, and new costumes can be 'broken down' with paint to make them look worn, as with Cinderella's rags.

Cutting

A tutu may take a day and a half to make. First, patterns are chalked onto the fabric and cut out by skilled dressmakers.

Sewing

The costume is tacked together with hand stitches, then sewn on a machine. Fastenings and trimmings are usually sewn on by hand.

Fitting

The half-finished costume is fitted on the dancer and any alterations made. A label is sewn into the costume and the dancer's name written in. Each costume can last many years and be worn by many dancers.

▲ **Nijinsky's costume in Petrushka, designed by Alexandre Benois for Diaghilev's Ballets Russes**

◀ **Odile's tutu, Swan Lake**

Repairs

When Vaslav Nijinsky danced in Fokine's Le Spectre de la Rose in 1911, his costume was sewn with petals in dusky pinks and browns to suggest the spirit of the rose. The costume constantly needed repairs because admirers of this great dancer took the petals as souvenirs.

▶ Dancing chickens in Frederick Ashton's ballet La Fille mal Gardée

▼ Costume for Jeremy Fisher in Frederick Ashton's Tales of Beatrix Potter

◀ Ian Spurling designed colourful and witty costumes for Kenneth MacMillan's ballet Elite Syncopations, which is set to ragtime music by Scott Joplin.

However elaborate the designs are, the dancers must still be able to move freely, lift their arms, turn and jump in the costumes. A costume must also complement the dancer's shape – tutus that are too long and droopy can make the dancer's legs look short and spoil the choreography. A design can suggest a character without the costume being realistic.

Make-up

Odette
Under strong stage lighting, dancers' features disappear unless they are made up quite heavily.

Siegfried
Men wear make-up too.

Von Rothbart
Swan Lake's wicked magician wears a fantasty make-up using many colours.

31

A dancer's diary

I still can't believe how quickly things have happened. One day it seemed as if I was going to be in the corps de ballet forever; the next day I had been cast for a leading role in a new full-length ballet. The choreographer was looking for someone new and liked my dancing. Since then, in some ways everything has changed, in others it's still the same and always will be.

"Like this..."

Business as usual

For instance, every morning at ten-thirty I have class for ninety minutes, and the teacher still corrects my mistakes. No chance of getting big-headed! At the moment I'm working on my travelling turns, which can go a bit wobbly as I cross the stage en diagonale. After class I rehearse all day, as I have lots of new ballerina roles to learn: Juliet and Cinderella this year, Aurora and Giselle next year.

Sometimes these are solo or pas de deux rehearsals, other times it's a full call with all the company, either in the studio or on stage. I'm very fortunate because the répétiteurs who coach me in these roles are usually famous dancers themselves, who pass on their knowledge to me. There are regular costume fittings now, and each week I collect my new pointe shoes and prepare them. I use so many these days – at least three pairs a week – that I seem to be constantly sewing on ribbons.

I have to remember to fit meals in somewhere, usually salad and fruit for lunch, something to give me energy just before the show, and something a bit more substantial afterwards. I might go out with my friends for pasta and my favourite pudding. Now that I'm a principal, I usually perform on stage only once or twice a week. On the other nights I might go to the theatre or see a film – I learn so much from watching others perform.

a new role

Fame

When I was dancing the Sugar Plum Fairy in The Nutcracker last Christmas, I was interviewed for children's television and answered a phone-in about ballet. Then, when I first became a principal dancer, several daily newspapers wanted to interview me. Journalists always ask if I'm nervous before a performance. Of course! Everyone is, but as soon as you see the audience and start dancing it just disappears. Now the whole world suddenly seems to be interested in me! I've modelled clothes for a Paris fashion designer and have just been photographed for a new book about ballet.

with the physiotherapist

Injury

It's not all fun, though. Last year I had a stress fracture which took a long time to heal. I hated being injured but at least it gave me time to catch up on replying to letters from people who have enjoyed my dancing. Thanks to the company physiotherapist, I'm now fully recovered.

Going on tour

I'm glad I didn't miss the company's tour of Japan and Korea. We took a triple bill, a programme of three short ballets: Les Sylphides, Les Patineurs and Danses Concertantes. When we arrive in a different theatre, there isn't usually time for a full stage rehearsal. Instead, the corps de ballet have a 'placing call' to see how they fit on the new stage – they pretend to be dancing but just walk through all their movements and groupings. The principals also walk through their steps on stage and without music, which is called 'marking'. On tour we often have a first-night celebration – it's good to meet members of the audience and talk to them about the performance. Then it's back to the hotel to wash our practice clothes ready for class in the morning.

Dancing in the USA

I have been asked to appear as a guest artist with one of the best ballet companies in the USA. The ballet they want me to dance is Balanchine's Stars and Stripes, with Sousa's marching music.

Stars and Stripes

Stars and Stripes is not in our repertoire. So I'll need to rehearse with them and fit into their production. One of the performances will be a Gala for the President. I'm sure they'll all make me very welcome. Then it's back to London and straight into class again, where I'll be working on those pirouettes. Back to earth with a bump!

curtain call

A ballerina's year

January: Performances of The Nutcracker – Sugar Plum Fairy solo filmed for children's television.

February: Rehearsals and costume fittings for new ballet.

March: First performance of new ballet. Radio and television interviews.

April: Tour of Far East (Japan and Korea). Rehearsals for Swan Lake.

May: Return to UK. Performances of Swan Lake. Rehearsals for Romeo and Juliet.

July: Romeo and Juliet televised live. Interviews for newspapers and magazines .

August: Holiday. No class or rehearsals.

September: Classes, rehearsals and coaching for Stars and Stripes.

October: Guest artist in US Gala Performance of Stars and Stripes.

November: Rehearsals for Cinderella. New partner joins company from Paris Opéra Ballet.

December: Performances of Cinderella. Meet audience after children's matinée.

PERFORMANCE

Golden lights glow in the auditorium. The heavy stage curtains are closed. People are talking quietly and reading their programmes. There are ripples of music as musicians tune up in the orchestra pit. The lights grow dim and silence falls. The conductor enters and steps on to the podium. He lifts his baton – the audience seems to hold its breath. Then the orchestra begins to play the overture, lively music that sets the scene. Everyone listens. Suddenly the curtain sweeps up and the stage is full of movement, colour and light.

Rudolf Nureyev saw his first ballet when he was seven. His family was very poor, and his mother could afford only one ticket. She took Rudolf and his three sisters along to the theatre in the cold Russian winter, and in the last-minute rush before the doors were closed, she managed to squeeze the whole family into the theatre. The experience was to change his life.

"I shall never forget a single detail of the scene which met my eyes; the theatre itself with its soft, beautiful lights and gleaming crystal chandeliers; small lanterns hanging everywhere; coloured windows; everywhere velvet, gold – another world; a place which, to my dazzled eyes, you could only hope to encounter in the most enchanted fairy tale. I was speechless. From that day I can truthfully date my unwavering decision to become a ballet dancer."
(Nureyev)

Swan Lake Act III

The evil Von Rothbart and his daughter, Odile, arrive at the ball, intent on deceiving Prince Siegfried. Odile has disguised herself as Odette, the beautiful Swan Princess whom Siegfried has promised to marry.

The stage manager runs the show. She calls dancers from their dressing rooms to the stage, and works closely with the stage crew and front-of-house staff to make sure everything runs smoothly.

The lighting desk is usually front-of-house, at the back of the auditorium. Technicians keep contact with backstage crew via a sound-system and TV monitors.

Curtain up

 The performance has begun. While the audience watches the ballet and listens to the music, behind the scenes everyone is hard at work, making the performance look as effortless as possible.

In the pit

The conductor uses the baton to show the orchestra how fast to play and to help them play together. He must also closely watch the dancers on stage and be aware of their needs.

In the interval, the audience can relax, talk about the ballet and read their programmes. Backstage in their dressing rooms, the dancers hastily change costumes, shoes and hairstyles. On stage, while the curtains are closed, stage crew quickly and quietly change the scenery, ready for the next act.

The dresser is in the dressing room of the principal ballerina, checking her costume for when she will appear as Odette in the next act.

In the wings, a dancer from the Neapolitan duet gets her breath back. The other dancer checks her shoes before going on as the vision of Odette in the window of the ballroom.

The stage technicians are responsible for sound, lighting, scenery, props and special effects. A large theatre may need a team of over 100 people.

Behind the scenes

Staging a ballet involves long-term planning, as far as five years ahead of the first performance. So while Swan Lake is under way, preparations have already begun for the next production. In a large theatre like the Met, work never stops.

1 Billboards advertise Swan Lake and other performances. The marketing and press departments design programmes, posters and leaflets to promote performances.
2 The foyer or entrance lobby where the audience gathers.
3 Bars and a restaurant sell refreshments.
4 The auditorium seats 3,800 on four tiers and an orchestra level.
5 Ballet rehearsal room.
6 Offices – administration, press and marketing.
7 The orchestra pit holds up to 110 musicians and can be raised to stage level for concerts.
8 The corps de ballet.
9 The principal dancers, Siegfried and Odette.
10 A spotlight operated by a lighting technician follows the principal dancers with a small pool of light. It isn't visible here, but the lighting and sound control booth is at the back of the auditorium on the orchestra level.

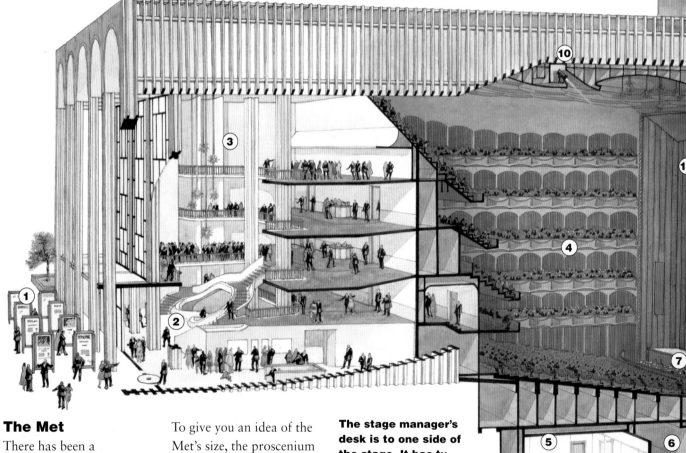

The Met

There has been a Metropolitan Opera House in New York since 1883. The New House at Lincoln Center opened in 1966, and presents both opera and ballet.

To give you an idea of the Met's size, the proscenium arch that frames the stage is the tallest in the world – it is 16.45m high. To run a theatre this big takes a big team of people – the Met employs about 1,000.

The stage manager's desk is to one side of the stage. It has tv monitors showing the stage and the conductor. An audio system calls dancers to the stage, cues front-of-house staff, and communicates with technicians.

11 The stage curtain.

12 The proscenium.

13 Lights are hung from four steel bridges above the stage. These bridges are big enough to hold the technicians who change the lights.

14 The backcloth, also known as the backdrop, is hung from the flies.

15 The backcloth for Act III waits to be lowered in the scene change during the interval.

16 On either side of the stage, there are five fly galleries for lighting and clearing scenery.

17 The fly system uses over 100 battens of steel tubing for hanging the

backcloths and scenery, and is electronically controlled. Older theatres use weights and pulleys and more manpower.

18 The main stage is 30m wide and 25m deep. It has seven hydraulically operated platforms which can be raised and lowered separately.

19 The rear slip stage, with a revolving platform that is 18m in diameter.

20 The right slip stage, where scenery for the next act or for another production can be set up and slid into place. (The left slip stage is on the other side of the stage.)

21 Scenery from Act I.

22 The loading dock can take four trucks at a time, to load or unload scenery.

23 Opera rehearsal room.

24 In the chorus dressing-room, each person has a place to make up at, with a mirror.

25 The carpentry workshop makes scenery and props. The scenery is painted in another area known as the paint shop, and is then taken by lift down to an underground storage area.

26 The electrical workshop does the heavy-duty metalwork for scenery and props, and maintains lighting, sound and electronic equipment.

27 A wardrobe holding area stores and maintains costumes for current productions.

28 The wig room is part of the costume shop, where new costumes are made, trimmed and fitted.

29 The principals each have a dressing-room with a shower, a sofa, a piano, and an audio paging system linked to the stage manager's desk.

Step by step

Watch for the patterns the steps make. They may be repeated several times, or one dancer will dance a step while the other seems to reply, like a conversation. Sometimes a group of dancers performs one series of steps together, while the soloist dances another in contrast or counterpoint. The same step can be danced in many different ways. All the different steps make up a dance vocabulary, which is the choreographer's tool kit.

WITHOUT WORDS

People going to their first ballet may worry whether they'll understand it. But as soon as the curtain goes up, they are swept along in the excitement. Most of the older ballets, such as Swan Lake, are narrative ballets – they tell stories. Acting, mime and large group scenes help to move the action along. Some ballets have no story but instead have a clear theme or idea.

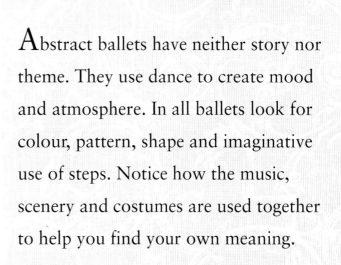

▶ Les Sylphides is a ballet in the Romantic style, but it was choreographed by Michel Fokine and first performed in 1909. It is a ballet with a theme but no story, and is set in moonlight near a ruined chapel.

Abstract ballets have neither story nor theme. They use dance to create mood and atmosphere. In all ballets look for colour, pattern, shape and imaginative use of steps. Notice how the music, scenery and costumes are used together to help you find your own meaning.

▲ Danses Concertantes is a lively modern ballet choreographed by Kenneth MacMillan to music by Stravinsky. It has no story or theme, but the unusual movements follow the music to make a ballet full of wit and fun. In this production, Ian Spurling's designs suggest a pool.

Moods and movement

To help you enjoy ballet more, ask yourself some questions as you watch. Are the dancers moving with strong leaping steps across the stage on their own, or with small neat steps within a large group? Do they use sudden darting steps or long slow stretching movements? What do these movements and groupings tell us?

Fun

Frederick Ashton's ballet The Dream is based on Shakespeare's play, A Midsummer Night's Dream.

The naughty sprite Puck uses quick light travelling steps. Here, he turns his palms upwards mischievously with his toe just touching the ground.

Joy

In Kenneth MacMillan's version of Shakespeare's play, Romeo and Juliet dance a joyful pas de deux in the garden beneath Juliet's balcony. She trusts him to support her in this difficult lift.

You can also use the clues given by the music, costumes, scenery and lighting. Is the stage dark and mysteriously blue or is it bright and sunny? What do the dancers' costumes tell you about their character or mood? Does the music emphasize the movement or provide an unusual contrast? What are you feeling as you watch?

Fear

Prince Ivan captures the Firebird in Fokine's ballet. He holds her tightly as if to stop her wings fluttering as she tries to escape. She looks fearfully back at him over her shoulder. Crossed positions with limbs turned inwards often show fear or sadness, while open positions show happiness or trust.

Sorrow

Petrushka, the unloved and unhappy puppet, kneels in misery with shoulders hunched and hands crossed. His head is tilted and his eyes look helplessly upwards.

Mime from Giselle

Gesture and expression help to tell the story:
1 Giselle, Act I: "I can **hear** Albrecht coming to meet me."
2 Albrecht, Act I: "I **promise** to **love** you forever, Giselle."
3 Princess Bathilde, Act I: "I am engaged to **marry** Albrecht."
4 Myrthe, the Queen of the Wilis, Act II: "You shall **die**, Albrecht !"
5 Albrecht, Act II: "**Why** must I die? Have pity!"

Telling a story

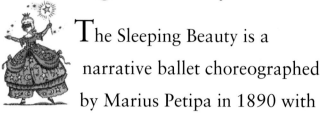

The Sleeping Beauty is a narrative ballet choreographed by Marius Petipa in 1890 with music by Tchaikovsky. Petipa based the ballet on the Charles Perrault fairy tale and made it in four sections – a prologue and three acts.

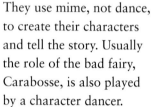

1 Danced by a soloist, the Lilac Fairy leads the fairies bringing gifts to the royal christening in the prologue. The King and Queen are character parts.

They use mime, not dance, to create their characters and tell the story. Usually the role of the bad fairy, Carabosse, is also played by a character dancer.

3 In Act I, Princess Aurora pricks her finger on the spindle and collapses. She is surrounded by the King and Queen, courtiers and suitors. This is a dramatic scène d'action.

Thanks to the Lilac Fairy, Aurora is not dead, only in a deep sleep.

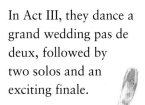

4 The roles of Aurora and Florimund are played by principal dancers, a prima ballerina and a premier danseur. Florimund finds the castle in Act II and wakes Aurora with a kiss.

In Act III, they dance a grand wedding pas de deux, followed by two solos and an exciting finale.

2 Angry at being left out of the christening, Carabosse uses mime to cast a spell: Aurora will prick her finger on a spindle and die. In some productions, Carabosse is played by a man.

5 Puss-in-Boots and the White Cat are usually danced by coryphées or junior soloists. These are called demi-caractère parts. They dance one of the divertissements during the wedding in Act III.

The Sleeping Beauty follows a pattern common to Petipa's other narrative ballets – ballets which tell a story. There are the scènes d'action, which tell the story clearly in acting and mime. Then there are pas d'action, which use dance steps to show what the characters are feeling. As the story unfolds, it is interrupted by divertissements, displays of dancing for its own sake which are not really part of the story. Finally there are variations, solos which highlight a dancer's virtuoso skills.

Tales from the Ballet

La Sylphide
First performed in 1836, in Copenhagen. Choreography: August Bournonville. Music: Herman von Løvenskjold

James is a young Scottish farmer. On the eve of his wedding to Effie, a beautiful sylphide (a fairy of the forest) appears at his window. James is now torn between his love for the Sylphide and for Effie. A witch called Madge tells Effie and her friends their fortunes – but James throws Madge out. The wedding is celebrated with Highland dancing, but just as the rings are about to be exchanged, the Sylphide entices James away. Effie is in despair.

Madge gives James a magic scarf, to capture the Sylphide. In the forest, James and the Sylphide dance with the scarf, but then James wraps it round her and pulls her to him. The angry witch has poisoned the scarf, and the Sylphide's wings fall from her body. Without them, she will die.

Giselle
1841, Paris
choreography: Jean Coralli and Jules Perrot
music: Adolphe Adam

Giselle loves 'Loys', who is Count Albrecht in disguise – a forester, Hilarion, is bitterly jealous. As they dance, her mother warns she might overtire herself and die, just like the Wilis – the ghosts of girls who died before their wedding day. The duke and his daughter, Bathilde, arrive with a hunting party. Giselle dances for them, and discovers that 'Loys' is engaged to Bathilde. She dances wildly, then dies at her mother's feet.

The Wilis rise from their graves, led by Myrtha, their Queen, and dance in the moonlight. Hilarion comes to Giselle's grave, and the Wilis make him dance to his death. Albrecht is also commanded to dance, but Giselle, now a Wili herself, dances for him. At dawn she returns to her grave, and Albrecht is spared.

Don Quixote
1869, Moscow
choreography: Marius Petipa
music: Ludwig Minkus

There are several versions of this ballet, based on a Spanish novel by Cervantes. Don Quixote is an old man bewitched by tales of knights in shining armour, and searches for similar adventures of his own.

In current productions, the main characters are the young lovers Basilio and Kitri, who live in Barcelona. Kitri is being forced by her father to marry rich Gamache. Don Quixote arrives at her father's inn, sees that Kitri is unhappy, and challenges Gamache to a duel – but the would-be knight is chased away. Basilio pretends he is dying, and begs Kitri's father to take pity and grant him permission to marry her – his wish is granted.

During the wedding celebrations, Basilio and Kitri perform a grand pas de deux, in Spanish style, and the ever-hopeful Don Quixote departs for further adventures.

Coppélia

1870, Paris
choreography:
Arthur Saint-Léon
music: Léo Delibes

Franz and Swanhilda live in a small town where Dr Coppélius has a toyshop. His favourite doll, Coppélia, is so lifelike that Franz falls in love with her. Furious, Swanhilda creeps into the shop with her friends to investigate.

Suddenly Dr Coppélius returns, so Swanhilda hides and changes into the doll's clothes. Franz climbs up a ladder to look at Coppélia. Dr Coppélius grabs him, and with magic spells tries to use Franz's energy to make the doll come alive. Swanhilda pretends she is Coppélia and performs a Scottish and a Spanish dance. Then she sets all the clockwork toys to work, to wake Franz. They escape, leaving a heartbroken Dr Coppélius.

As the town celebrates a new bell with Dances of the Hours, Dawn and Prayer, Swanhilda apologizes to Dr Coppélius for her deception and dances with Franz.

The Sleeping Beauty

1890, St Petersburg
choreography: Petipa
music: Pytor Ilyich
Tchaikovsky

See pages 44–45.

The Nutcracker

1892, Moscow
choreography: Lev Ivanov
music: Tchaikovsky

It is Christmas in Germany. A mysterious guest arrives at the Stahlbaums' party. It is Herr Drosselmeyer, with a soldier's uniform for Fritz, and a nutcracker for Clara in the shape of a soldier.

After the party, Clara creeps downstairs to fetch her nutcracker. Drosselmeyer appears, the clock stops, and the Christmas Tree and the toys grow huge and come alive. The Nutcracker does battle with the evil Mouse King, and Drosselmeyer changes him into a prince who takes Clara on a magical journey.

First, they travel to the Land of Snow where they meet the Snow Queen. Then they visit the Land of Sweets, where the Sugar Plum Fairy presents a series of divertissements for Clara: a coffee dance, a tea dance, Madame Bonbonnière, a Russian dance, and lastly the Waltz of the Flowers. The Prince and the Sugar Plum Fairy dance solos and a grand pas de deux before Clara suddenly finds herself back at home, wondering if it was all a dream.

Swan Lake

1877, Moscow
choreography: Acts
I and III by Petipa,
II and IV by Ivanov
music: Tchaikovsky

It is Prince Siegfried's 21st birthday. His mother tells him he must soon be married. He sets off to the forest.

By a lake deep in the forest, Siegfried sees a swan and takes aim to shoot, but the swan becomes a beautiful girl. She begs Siegfried not to shoot – she is Princess Odette and she and her companions have been turned into swans by Von Rothbart, an evil magician disguised as an owl. Only true love will save her. The Prince promises to love and marry her. ➡

Siegfried vows never to break his promise. They and the other swan-maidens dance until Von Rothbart draws them back to the lake and under his spell.

The Queen arranges a ball and several princesses dance, but the Prince rejects them all. Suddenly a mysterious guest arrives. It is Von Rothbart in disguise with his daughter, Odile. Siegfried thinks she is Odette. As they dance together, Siegfried declares he will love her forever. A vision of Odette appears at the window, Von Rothbart and Odile laugh triumphantly, and Siegfried realizes he has been tricked into breaking his promise to Odette.

Odette and the other swan-maidens are dancing sadly by the lake. Siegfried arrives and begs Odette to forgive him, which she does. But Von Rothbart now has the swan-maidens in his power forever. In desperation, Siegfried and Odette throw themselves in the lake, and at last the spell is broken by the power of their love for one another.

The Firebird
1910, Paris
choreography:
Michel Fokine
music: Igor Stravinsky

The evil magician Kotschei has imprisoned a Princess and her 11 companions in an enchanted garden. Prince Ivan climbs over the wall and, seeing a beautiful Firebird, captures her. In exchange for her release, she gives him one of her feathers, promising to return if ever he is in danger. Ivan hides to watch the princess as she dances with her friends, with golden apples they shake from the trees. He falls in love with her but is captured by Kotschei and his hideous creatures. Ivan summons the Firebird, who shows him how to destroy the magician by smashing a large egg containing his soul. Kotschei's creatures are now freed from the spell that has imprisoned them. Ivan and the princess are crowned king and queen amid great celebration by all who were once Kotschei's prisoners.

Petrushka
1911, Paris
choreography: Fokine
music: Stravinsky

It is Butterweek Fair in St Petersburg, Russia. A Showman is there, with three lifesize puppets – a Ballerina, a Moor and a clown called Petrushka. They perform for the crowds.

When the show is over and the puppets are back in their booths, the Ballerina makes fun of Petrushka and the Showman ill-treats him. In his frustration, Petrushka beats his fists on the wall of his booth.

The Ballerina visits the Moor, followed by jealous Petrushka. The Moor chases Petrushka out of the booth and strikes him with a scimitar. To the crowd's horror, Petrushka appears to bleed, but the Showman lifts up the limp body and shows them it is only a puppet, leaking sawdust.

As night falls and the Fair closes, the ghost of Petrushka rises above the sideshow, taunting the Showman.

Cinderella
1948, London
choreography:
Frederick Ashton
music: Sergei Prokofiev

Cinderella's two ugly stepsisters (men dressed up as women, in pantomime tradition) set out for the palace ball, leaving Cinderella behind. In rags, with her broom as partner, she dreams of dancing. Suddenly her Fairy Godmother arrives with the fairies of the four seasons. She casts magic spells so that Cinderella can go to the ball in a beautiful dress – but she must come home at midnight.

At the ball, Cinderella descends the staircase en pointe and dances with the Prince. On the stroke of midnight she rushes out, losing one of her slippers. The Prince vows to marry the girl whose foot it fits.

Back home, the Ugly Sisters try to squash their huge feet into the tiny slipper. Cinderella shyly tries the slipper – it fits, and the Prince marries her, to the dismay of the Ugly Sisters.

La Fille mal Gardée
1960, London
choreography:
Ashton
music: Ferdinand Hérold, arranged by John Lanchbery.

Lise and her mother, Widow Simone (played by a man), live on a farm in France. Lise is in love with Colas, and they dance together with a long ribbon. Widow Simone introduces Alain, son of wealthy Farmer Thomas, but Lise is not impressed.

At the harvest, Lise and Colas dance with their friends, Widow Simone does a comical clog dance, and then everyone dances round a maypole.

Back at home, harvesters bring in sheaves of wheat. Colas jumps out from the wheat, and Lise hides him in her room. Widow Simone brings Alain to marry Lise, and Colas is discovered. Widow Simone finally relents, and agrees to Lise marrying Colas. The house empties, and Alain creeps in to fetch his beloved red umbrella.

Romeo and Juliet
1965, London
choreography:
Kenneth MacMillan
music: Prokofiev

This ballet is based on Shakespeare's play. Two families in Verona, Italy, have been ordered to end their feud. The Montagues have a son, Romeo. The Capulets have a daughter, Juliet, and a nephew, Tybalt. At a masked ball, Romeo falls in love with Juliet. They meet beneath Juliet's balcony and declare their love for each other.

In a small chapel, with her nurse-maid as witness, Romeo and Juliet are married. But fighting breaks out, Tybalt kills a friend of Romeo, so Romeo kills Tybalt and flees the city.

Juliet's parents have arranged for her to marry Paris. In despair, she takes a drug that will make her look dead, when really only asleep.

The Capulets discover Juliet's body and lay her in the family vault. Romeo rushes in. Thinking Juliet is dead, he takes poison. Juliet wakes to find her beloved Romeo dead at her side, and stabs herself.

Enjoying ballet

You don't have to go to ballet classes to enjoy ballet. There are lots of other ways to be a knowledgeable ballet fan.

Watching ballet

You can start by watching ballet on television and video. You will enjoy it much more if you read the story first and listen to some of the music.

▼ Meeting dancers and collecting autographs after the show.

Ask yourself questions about what you see. Was it well danced? If so, what made it special? What if it wasn't so good? What might have made it better?

Keeping a scrapbook

You can fill a scrapbook with cuttings about ballet and pictures of your favourite dancers clipped from newspapers, magazines and publicity material.

Writing a review

Look out for reviews by critics who write about the performances.

Try to write your own brief review of a ballet you have seen. Imagine you are writing it for someone who has never seen a ballet before. How would you describe it for them?

Going to the theatre

If you want to watch ballet live, you can start with performances by local ballet schools. When a professional ballet company visits your local theatre, try to see the performance. If you go in a group with friends from school or your ballet class, the tickets are usually cheaper. Companies sometimes have talks before the performance, to help explain what you are about to see.

Ballet companies usually have an education officer who will be happy to tell you what they offer – anything from booklets and posters for sale to a place in a workshop where you can learn some of the choreography. You can telephone or write to them at the theatre where the company is based.

Workshops

Workshops teach you basic ballet movements, and sometimes help you use these to create your own dances.

Your teacher at school may be able to arrange for dancers from a company to visit, talk about their lives, dance and teach a workshop.

If you are already dancing, there are summer schools where you can make friends with other dancers, have classes with different teachers, take part in a performance, or try your hand at choreography.

▼ A school visit by a ballet company may include a workshop on make-up and costume. Kostchei, the evil magician in The Firebird, wears a great fantasy make-up.

Design your own ballet

Don't forget that ballet is four things in one – dance, music, art and drama. If you are interested in costume and design, you might like to choose a story and make drawings of ballet scenery and costumes.

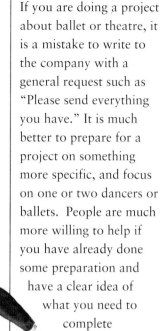

▲ **A school workshop on pas de deux**

If you play an instrument, get together with others and compose some ballet music. You can use a computer to do both of these. Make a cassette or video recording of your work.

If you want to know more about ballet history and famous dancers, use your library – it may lend tapes and videos too.

There are also museums that display costumes, such as Anna Pavlova's Swan tutu, and designs and scores from Diaghilev's company.

Ballet in art

Painters, sculptors and photographers have always been fascinated by ballet.

Look out for exhibitions of work by painters such as Degas, Dame Laura Knight and Robert Heindel or photographs by Cecil Beaton, Richard Avedon and Anthony Crickmay. You might like to sketch or paint ballet yourself, or use clay to capture those elusive positions.

Whatever you choose to do, it will help you to enjoy and understand ballet more.

Finding out

If you are doing a project about ballet or theatre, it is a mistake to write to the company with a general request such as "Please send everything you have." It is much better to prepare for a project on something more specific, and focus on one or two dancers or ballets. People are much more willing to help if you have already done some preparation and have a clear idea of what you need to complete your project.

Every major theatre has its own archive, which is like a museum or library and is looked after by an archivist. The archive might include old books, posters, programmes, reviews, costumes, photographs and choreographers' notes.

If you are interested in a particular dancer, choreographer or ballet, you can write to the archivist for specific information. Sometimes it is even possible to arrange a visit to the archive and see its treasures for yourself.

▼ **Pavlova Taking A Bow, by Dame Laura Knight (1877–1970). Knight loved to paint scenes from the ballet and the circus.**

Great dancers of the 20th century

Mikhail Baryshnikov

See page 11.

Darcey Bussell

Born in London in 1969, Bussell trained at The Royal Ballet School and became a principal with the company in 1989. Her dancing combines great virtuosity with a fresh, youthful quality – as in her Aurora for The Royal Ballet's new production of The Sleeping Beauty, which was premiered in Washington in 1994.

Erik Bruhn

This dancer was known for his superb technique and elegant manner in classical roles, and was one of the very best male dancers. Born in 1928, Bruhn trained at the Royal Danish Ballet School, joining the company in 1937. He danced in the UK, USA and Denmark, and directed in Sweden and Canada. He also encouraged dancers to take more responsibility for their well-being and careers. He died in 1986.

Suzanne Farrell

Born in 1945, Farrell trained at the American School of Ballet and joined New York City Ballet at 16. As an NYCB star, she was known for her immaculate technique and extensions in adage. She danced in many ballets choreographed by George Balanchine, including Jewels, Variations and Union Jack. Her most famous partnership was with Peter Martins, who joined the company in 1969.

Margot Fonteyn

Romeo and Juliet

Born in Britain in 1919, Fonteyn studied at Dame Ninette de Valois' Sadler's Wells school, becoming a soloist with the company at 16. She is remembered for her flawless classical technique and her beauty and elegance as a ballerina. Famous partners include Michael Somes and Rudolf Nureyev, and famous performances include Swan Lake, The Sleeping Beauty, Romeo and Juliet, and Marguerite and Armand. Honoured with the titles Dame and Prima Ballerina Assoluta, Fonteyn died in 1991.

Sylvie Guillem

Born in 1965, Guillem trained at the Paris Opéra Ballet School, from which she graduated into the company. She is a principal guest artist with The Royal Ballet but also appears with other companies. As a child, Guillem trained as a gymnast and is known for her extensions and suppleness – Royal Opera House audiences were amazed by her performances in American choreographer William Forsythe's ballets – In the Middle Somewhat Elevated and Herman Schmerman.

Marcia Haydée

Born in Brazil in 1939, this ballerina created many leading roles for the Stuttgart Ballet under the direction of choreographer John Cranko. She was known for her lyrical dancing and powerful acting in such ballets as The Taming of the Shrew and Eugene Onegin. She retired as Stuttgart's Artistic Director in 1996.

Karen Kain

Born in 1951, she trained at the National Ballet School in Canada, joining the company in 1969. She became a principal dancer in 1971 and has appeared as guest artist with many other leading companies. Kain was one of Nureyev's celebrated partners.

Irek Mukhamedov

Mukhamedov trained at the Bolshoi Ballet school, and as a leading dancer with the company was famous for dramatic roles in ballets such as Spartacus. In 1990 he joined The Royal Ballet. He is known for his great technical skill and superb acting and has danced in new ballets by a variety of choreographers.

Vaslav Nijinsky

Born in Russia in 1889, Nijinsky trained at the Imperial Russian Ballet School. He joined Diaghilev's Ballets Russes where he had a short but legendary career, dancing in ballets such as Le Spectre de la Rose, Petrushka and The Firebird. He also danced and choreographed two sensational ballets, The Rite of Spring

The Rite of Spring

and L'Après-midi d'un Faune. Nijinsky suffered from mental illness and died in hospital in 1950. His diaries and a biography written by his wife give a fascinating insight into his life and the times in which he danced.

Rudolf Nureyev

Born in 1938 on a train journey in Russia, Nureyev trained at the Leningrad Ballet School from the age of 17 and at 20 made his debut with the Kirov Ballet. In 1961, Nureyev left a tour with the Kirov and was invited to join The Royal Ballet. He danced many leading roles, establishing a famous partnership with Margot Fonteyn, and was a virtuoso performer with a magnetic personality. He also choreographed new productions of well-known ballets such as The Nutcracker, Don Quixote and Romeo and Juliet. Nureyev became Director of the Paris Opéra Ballet in 1983 and died in 1993.

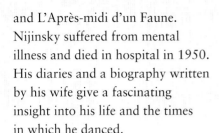

The Nutcracker

Anna Pavlova

See pages 10-11.

Galina Ulanova

Born in Russia in 1910, this great ballerina danced with both the Kirov and the Bolshoi Ballet Companies, and was known for her graceful and poignant performances in ballets such as Giselle. Ulanova went on to teach at the Bolshoi Ballet School, coaching students for ballerina roles. She died in 1998.

Great teachers

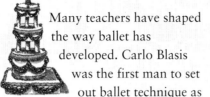

Many teachers have shaped the way ballet has developed. Carlo Blasis was the first man to set out ballet technique as we know it today, in a book called The Code of Terpsichore, which was published in 1830. August Bournonville led the Royal Danish Ballet from 1830 and created its unique technique of ballet, including ballon – very light, springy jumping. Many schools, especially in Eastern Europe, study the method named after Agrippina Vaganova, a Russian teacher who died in 1951. Other dancers study the Cecchetti method, named after Enrico Cecchetti who taught many famous dancers of the Maryinsky and Diaghilev companies – including Anna Pavlova.

Great composers

Jean Baptiste Lully 1632–1687 One of the first composers for ballet at the court of Louis XIV was a dancer himself and became Director of the Académie Royale de Musique. His ballets include Le Ballet de la Nuit, with Louis XIV as the sun god Apollo.

Léo Delibes 1836–1891 A French composer much admired by Tchaikovsky, Delibes composed La Source, Sylvia and Coppélia. In Coppélia, he developed the idea of motif begun by Adam in Giselle – a motif is a musical theme for each character.

Frédéric Chopin 1810–1849. Born in Poland, Chopin wrote no ballet music as such, but his music has been used for many ballets. The best-known is probably Les Sylphides (called Chopiniana at first), which was choreographed by Fokine. Jerome Robbins used Chopin's music for The Concert and Dances at a Gathering, as did Ashton for A Month in the Country.

Sergei Prokofiev 1891–1953 Prokofiev's ballet music includes Prodigal Son, The Stone Flower, Cinderella, and Romeo and Juliet. This Russian classical composer also wrote operas and film scores.

Igor Stravinsky 1882–1971 This Russian composer worked closely with Diaghilev, Nijinsky and Balanchine, and wrote music for ballets such as The Firebird, Petrushka, Les Noces, The Rite of Spring, Apollo and Agon. Music not specially written for ballet has been used by choreographers such as MacMillan and Robbins.

Pyotr Ilych Tchaikovsky 1840–1893 See page 26.

Great choreographers of the 20th century

Frederick Ashton

Born in Ecuador, South America, in 1904, Ashton studied with Léonide Massine and Marie Rambert. An outstanding choreographer, he was also Director of The Royal Ballet from 1963 to 1970. Audiences love his ballets for their lyricism, musicality and imaginative use of classical technique. The Cecchetti method forms the basis of much of his work. Narrative and theme ballets include Cinderella, Sylvia, La Fille mal Gardée, Ondine, The Dream, Enigma Variations, The Two Pigeons, and A Month in the Country. Abstract ballets include Symphonic Variations, Scènes de Ballet and Monotones. For children, Ashton choreographed the delightful Tales of Beatrix Potter. He had the gift of creating characters that came alive on stage, and many succesful dancers made their début in his ballets. Sir Frederick died in 1988.

La Fille mal Gardée

George Balanchine

Born in St Petersburg in 1904, Balanchine trained at the Petrograd Imperial Ballet Academy. Diaghilev made him chief choreographer of the Ballets Russes in 1925. He was invited to the USA, where he started the School of American Ballet in 1934, and one year later the best students formed a new company, American Ballet. His next company, The Ballet Society, was the nucleus from which New York City Ballet grew. Balanchine is one of the greatest choreographers in the history of ballet. His ballets are mostly abstract celebrations of dance, in which his dancers are able to show superb skill, musicality and the joy of dance. His works include Concerto Barocco, Theme and Variations, Agon, Apollo, Symphony in C and The Four Temperaments. Balanchine died in 1983, leaving a world-famous company with a strong, distinctive style.

Maurice Béjart

Born in France in 1927, Béjart founded the Ballet of the Twentieth Century in Brussels in 1960. His work is dramatic and controversial and draws its inspiration from theatre and dance from all over the world. He uses large group scenes to create powerful effects and choreographs particularly well for male dancers. His ballets include The Rite of Spring, Nijinsky – Clown of God, and Bolero, which is set to Ravel's hypnotic music. The company is now based in Lausanne, Switzerland.

John Cranko

Born in South Africa in 1927, Cranko trained at the Sadler's Wells Ballet School and joined the company in 1946. He became Director of the Stuttgart Ballet in 1961 and choreographed many lasting works for Stuttgart and for The Royal Ballet, including the full-length ballets The Taming of the Shrew and Romeo and Juliet, as well as shorter ballets such as Pineapple Poll and The Lady and the Fool. Cranko's work is known for its wit, humour and strong characterization. He died in 1973, leaving the Stuttgart company one of the strongest in Europe.

Apollo

Yuri Grigorovich

Born in Russia in 1927, Grigorovich became chief choreographer and artistic director of the Bolshoi Ballet in 1964. His work is full of strong athletic dancing for the men and elegant virtuoso steps for women. Using scenes from Russian history, he made epic ballets with large crowds and lyrical pas de deux. Such ballets include The Golden Age, set in the 1920s; Ivan the Terrible, set in 16th-century Russia; and Spartacus, about a slave rebellion in Roman times.

Kenneth MacMillan

Born in 1929, MacMillan originally trained as a dancer at the Sadler's Wells School.

Elite Syncopations

In 1946 MacMillan joined the Sadler's Wells Theatre Ballet. He later became a choreographer, and was appointed Resident Choreographer for The Royal Ballet in 1965 and Artistic Director in 1970. He is best known for full-length narrative ballets such as Romeo and Juliet, Anastasia, Manon and Mayerling. But he has also choreographed memorable abstract ballets such as Elite Syncopations, Song of the Earth and Gloria, which takes its theme from the grief caused by World War I. His ballets use classical technique and dramatic staging to convey complex human emotions, and have a powerful impact on the audience. Sir Kenneth died in 1992.

Bronislava Nijinska

Born in 1891 in Russia, Bronislava was the sister of Vaslav Nijinsky. She studied with Cecchetti and joined first the Maryinsky company and then the Ballets Russes. She choreographed numerous ballets, including Renard, Les Biches and one of the most outstanding, Les Noces. With music by Stravinsky, and designs by Russian painter Natalia Goncharova, Les Noces draws on preparations for a traditional Russian wedding for its theme. Although Bronislava used classical steps, she drew on folk and jazz influences to create ballets in which design, dance and music blend together to unusual effect.

Jerome Robbins

Born in the USA in 1918, Robbins began his career as a dancer in musicals on Broadway. His first ballet, Fancy Free, was set to music by Leonard Bernstein – featuring three sailors out to enjoy themselves. It was so successful that it became a stage and screen musical called On the Town. His classical works are enjoyable celebrations of dance such as The Concert and Dances at a Gathering, both created for New York City Ballet. But they can also be tense and powerful, like his version of Afternoon of a Faun (a translation of L'Apres-midi d'un Faune). This ballet is choreographed to the same Debussy score that Nijinsky used in 1912. Set in a ballet studio, it explores the relationship between two dancers. Robbins later won an Oscar for his collaboration with Bernstein on the film West Side Story, which was first staged as a musical.

Glen Tetley

Born in the USA in 1926, Tetley first studied

Voluntaries

medicine, then danced with Antony Tudor and Martha Graham. He began as a choreographer in the contemporary dance style, with works such as Pierrot Lunaire, and then produced more classical ballets, such as Field Figures and Voluntaries. His works are usually abstract, full of unusual and imaginative movement, shapes and patterns to music by some outstanding modern composers such as Varèse, Berg, Schoenberg and Henze.

Antony Tudor

Born in 1908, Tudor did not begin dancing until he was 19. He trained at the Rambert School, which was attached to the ballet company founded in the 1930s by Dame Marie Rambert. She had once been a member of Diaghilev's company, and she encouraged many young choreographers such as Ashton, Tudor and Cranko. Tudor's works had a strong dramatic element and were performed by Ballet Rambert, New York City Ballet, The Royal Ballet and The Royal Swedish Ballet. They include Lilac Garden, Pillar of Fire and Shadowplay. Pillar of Fire and his last ballet, Tiller of the Fields, were both created for American Ballet Theatre. Tudor died in 1987.

Ninette de Valois

De Valois was born in Ireland in 1898 and danced with Diaghilev. She founded the Vic-Wells Ballet in 1931, which led to the Sadler's Wells Theatre Ballet, from which grew The Royal Ballet and Birmingham Royal Ballet. Her works have strong national themes, are full of dramatic and rich choreography, and use British composers and designers. They include Job, Checkmate and The Rake's Progress, which is based on a series of 18th-century paintings by William Hogarth about the rise and fall of a young man-about-town. During her long career, de Valois was responsible for noticing and encouraging many other choreographers such as Ashton, Cranko, MacMillan and David Bintley. She died in 2001.

Great companies

American Ballet Theatre

After Anna Pavlova's partner, Mikhail Mordkin, toured his small company in the USA, some of his Russian dancers, led by Lucia Chase and Richard Pleasant, formed Ballet Theatre in 1939. The company (later named American Ballet Theatre) became a centre-piece of the American ballet tradition, with such guest dancers as Erik Bruhn, Natalia Makarova and Gelsey Kirkland. It has staged successful works by choreographers such as Mikhail Fokine, George Balanchine, Agnes de Mille, Glen Tetley, Twyla Tharp, Jerome Robbins and Antony Tudor. In 1980, Mikhail Baryshnikov became ABT's Director. The company is now led by Kevin Mckenzie.

Australian Ballet

The company as it is known today was founded by Ninette de Valois' assistant, Peggy van Praagh, in 1962. In 1965, Robert Helpmann, an early partner of Margot Fonteyn, became its Director. The company is based in Melbourne and has its own school. It presents strong productions of the classics as well as new work and tours worldwide.

Birmingham Royal Ballet

When it moved into Covent Garden in 1946, The Royal Ballet had a touring section which visited theatres all over Great Britain and abroad. In the 1970s part of this touring company was based once again at Sadler's Wells Theatre, where it was called The Sadler's Wells Royal Ballet, under the direction of Sir Peter Wright. In 1990, the company moved to Birmingham, where it is based at the Hippodrome in specially designed studios. David Bintley, choreographer of popular ballets such as The Snow Queen and Hobson's Choice, was appointed Director in 1995.

Bolshoi Theatre

Sydney Opera House

The Bolshoi Ballet

This world-famous Russian company probably began with a ballet class which opened at the Moscow orphanage in 1774 to provide dancers for the Petrovsky Theatre. The company has been based at the Bolshoi Theatre since 1856. Carlo Blasis taught at the school in the 1860s. The company performed the very first Swan Lake, and Marius Petipa created Don Quixote for it in 1869. The Bolshoi's dramatic and flamboyant style emerged in the 1930s, under the direction of Leonid Lavrovsky. The company now tours worldwide.

Dance Theatre of Harlem

This company, founded by former New York City Ballet principal dancer Arthur Mitchell and Karel Shook, was the first ballet company to develop black classical dancers. It was founded as a school in 1968 and made its debut in 1971 at the Guggenheim Museum in New York with three Mitchell ballets. The company went on to perform ballets by Balanchine, Tetley and Geoffrey Holder, as well as new versions of The Firebird (set on a tropical island) and Giselle (set in Louisiana).

English National Ballet

Dame Alicia Markova and Sir Anton Dolin, both former dancers with Diaghilev, gathered together a group of dancers in 1949. From this grew Festival Ballet, which had its first performance in 1950. In 1968 the company became known as London Festival Ballet. Performing regularly at the Festival Hall, the company toured widely. Early productions included Witch Boy, Peer Gynt and Etudes. Now called English National Ballet, the company is currently led by Matz Skoog, former director of the Royal New Zealand Ballet.

The Kirov Ballet

This renowned Russian company was founded in St Petersburg in 1783. By the late 1800s, the company was performing at the Maryinsky Theatre, drawing its pupils from the famous ballet academy in Theatre Street. Petipa produced The Sleeping Beauty, The Nutcracker, Swan Lake and Raymonda for the company.

At the turn of the century, its most famous dancers were Preobajenska, Pavlova, Karsavina and Nijinsky. The company survived the Russian Revolution and toured abroad. Under the direction of Sergeyev, the company emphasized the preservation of the classics, and lost many of its leading dancers such as Nureyev, Makarova and Baryshnikov to the West.

National Ballet of Canada

Founded in 1951 and based in Toronto, the company's first Director was Celia Franca, followed by Alexander Grant, both British dancers. Grant introduced Frederick Ashton's ballets into the wide repertoire. Danish star Erik Bruhn was Artistic Director from 1983 to 1986. There is a ballet school attached to the company.

New York City Ballet

American writer and arts patron Lincoln Kirstein invited George Balanchine to open a ballet school, with the dream of it becoming America's first ballet company. It began presenting ballets in New York in the 1940s, and in 1964 New York City Ballet moved into the State Theater at the Lincoln Center. Its great dancers include Jacques d'Amboise, Melissa Hayden, Maria Tallchief and Edward Villella. Although the Balanchine ballets are central to the company's repertoire, preserved by the Balanchine Trust, it performs many new works and is currently under the direction of

Metropolitan Opera House, New York

an outstanding former dancer and choreographer, Peter Martins. The New York City Ballet School is one of the most famous in the world.

Palais Garnier, Paris

Paris Opéra Ballet

The company can be traced back to Louis XIV and the Académie Royale de Danse, which opened a training establishment in 1713. Among the first stars were Camargo and Sallé, followed by Vestris and Noverre. Romantic ballerinas Taglioni and Elssler made their début at the Paris Opéra in the 1830s. The company moved to its present home in the Palais Garnier in 1875. Rudolf Nureyev directed the company from 1983 until his death. There is a school attached to the company, whose pupils were traditionally known as Les Petits Rats (the little rats).

The Royal Ballet

The company grew out of the Sadler's Wells Ballet School, founded at Sadler's Wells Theatre by Dame Ninette de Valois in the 1930s. At first it was called the Vic-Wells Ballet. In 1946 the company, then called the Sadler's Wells Theatre Ballet, moved into The Royal Opera House, Covent Garden, with a new production of The Sleeping Beauty. It gained a royal charter to

become The Royal Ballet in 1956. The company has a school attached to it, The Royal Ballet School, directed by Gailene Stock AM. Monica Mason OBE is the director of the Royal Ballet Company. These former ballerinas have transferred the strength and discipline learned during their ballet training to their latest roles, making them confident, clear-sighted leaders.

The Royal Opera House, Covent Garden

The Royal Danish Ballet

When this company was established in 1784, there had been court ballet in Denmark since the 16th century. August Bournonville, a student of Vestris, became ballet master in 1830. In control of both the school and the company, he was able to establish the distinctive style which still exists today. Bournonville ballets still cherished by the company include Napoli, La Sylphide and Konservatoriet, which recreates a ballet class with Vestris.

The Stuttgart Ballet

Choreographer Jean Georges Noverre was the first to lead this court ballet, from 1760 to 1766. More recently, it began to attract worldwide recognition with the appointment of John Cranko as Director in 1960 – this established its reputation for exciting and lively choreography. The school attached to the company is known for its high standards of technique.

Ballet in history

Ballet has changed a great deal through the ages. The changes were part of many other things that happened in history – how people lived, what battles they fought, even what they wore and ate.

1462 First known writing about dance technique, by Domenico di Piacenza. Italian courts hold lavish dance entertainments.

1581 The first known ballet, Le Ballet Comique de la Reine, is performed at a royal marriage in France, from 10pm to 3am.

1588 Arbeau's Orchesographie is the first French writing about dance technique.

1608 Cosimo de' Medici holds a horse ballet in Florence, Italy.

1620 Mayflower Pilgrims land in Massachusetts, America.

1642–1646 Civil War in England (Roundheads versus Cavaliers).

1653 Louis XIV dances as the sun god Apollo in Le Ballet Royal de la Nuit, France.

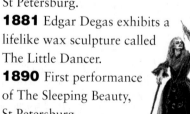

Louis XIV

1661 Louis XIV founds the Académie Royale de Danse, France.

1669 The Académie Royale de Musique is founded, France.

1681 First female dancers appear on stage in Jean Baptiste Lully's Le Triomphe de l'Amour, France. (One of the ballerinas, Mademoiselle de Lafontaine, is reputed to have danced for 10 years and then became a nun.)

1717 John Weaver's Loves of Mars and Venus is staged in London.

1727 Marie Camargo shortens her skirts, France.

1738 Imperial Ballet School is founded, in St Petersburg, Russia.

Marie Camargo

1758 Jean Georges Noverre produces two early ballets d'action, Les Caprices de Galathée and La Toilette de Venus, France.

1762 Catherine the Great becomes Empress of Russia.

1774 Bolshoi Ballet School is founded at an orphanage in Moscow, Russia.

1776 American Declaration of Independence.

1781 Noverre becomes ballet master at Kings Theatre, London.

1789 French Revolution begins.

1801 Salvatore Vigano presents Creatures of Prometheus in Vienna, with Beethoven's only ballet score.

1804 Napoleon is crowned Emperor of France.

1815 Battle of Waterloo.

1830 August Bournonville becomes ballet master of the Royal Danish Ballet. Carlo Blasis publishes The Code of Terpsichore in London.

1832 Marie Taglioni dances La Sylphide – the beginning of Romantic ballet. (Russian admirers later cook her shoes in a stew.)

1837 Coronation of Queen Victoria.

1840 Fanny Elssler is the first Romantic ballerina to tour America.

1841 First performance of Giselle, Paris.

1845 Four stars of Romantic ballet (Fanny Cerrito, Lucile Grahn, Carlotta Grisi and Marie Taglioni) dance their famous Pas de Quatre.

1861–1865 American Civil War.

1862 A rising star in Paris, Emma Livry refuses to wear the less-than-white but more flame-proof tutu – her skirts catch fire in rehearsal and she dies from her burns.

1869 Marius Petipa is appointed First Ballet Master to the Tsar's Imperial Ballet, St Petersburg. First performance of Don Quixote, Moscow.

1870 First performance of Coppélia, Paris. Franco-Prussian War begins – siege of Paris.

1877 First performance of Swan Lake, in Moscow, is not a success – but it will be revived in 1895 in St Petersburg.

1881 Edgar Degas exhibits a lifelike wax sculpture called The Little Dancer.

1890 First performance of The Sleeping Beauty, St Petersburg.

1892 First performance of The Nutcracker, St Petersburg.

Carabosse, in The Sleeping Beauty

1895 First performance of 32 fouettés in Swan Lake, by Pierina Legnani in St Petersburg.

1905 Mikhail Fokine choreographs a three-minute solo, The Dying Swan, for Anna Pavlova, Russia. Her costume uses real feathers.

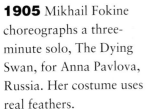

Pavlova

1909 First season of Serge Diaghilev's Ballets Russes, Paris – in the next two seasons, The Firebird and Petrushka will be smash hits.

1910 Léon Bakst designs Schéhérazade for Diaghilev, Paris.

1911 Alexandre Benois designs Petrushka for Diaghilev, Paris.

1913 First performance of Vaslav Nijinsky's Rite of Spring in Paris, to music by Igor Stravinsky – a riot breaks out in the theatre.

1914–1918 World War I.

Petrushka

1916 Ballet Russes performs in New York.

1917 Jean Cocteau designs Cubist ballet, Parade, for Diaghilev – music by Erik Satie (including ships' sirens and a typewriter) and choreography by Léonide Massine. Russian Revolution.

1919 Nijinsky's last performance.

1928 First performance of George Balanchine's Apollo, Paris.

1928 Women aged 21 and over able to vote in UK.

1929 Death of Diaghilev in Venice, Italy.

1931 Ninette de Valois becomes Director of Vic-Wells Ballet, London.

1934 Balanchine and Kirstein open School of American Ballet. Margot Fonteyn's first role is a snowflake in The Nutcracker – she will retire at the age of 60.

1939–1945 World War II.

1939 Ballet Theatre (later American Ballet Theatre) is founded. First performance by Ballet Rambert, founded by Marie Rambert, UK.

1940 First performance of Leonid Lavrovsky's Romeo and Juliet, Leningrad.

1944 First performance of Jerome Robbins's Fancy Free, by Ballet Theatre, USA.

1945 Balanchine choreographs a circus polka for elephants, to music by Stravinsky. Founding of the United Nations, New York.

1946 Sadler's Wells Ballet moves to Covent Garden, London.

1948 First performance of Frederick Ashton's Cinderella, London.

1950 Alicia Markova and Anton Dolin form Festival Ballet, London.

1951 National Ballet of Canada is founded, Toronto.

1953 Coronation of Queen Elizabeth II.

1956 Sadler's Wells Ballet becomes The Royal Ballet.

1957 Treaty of Rome establishes the European Community.

1960 John Cranko becomes Director of the Stuttgart Ballet. First performance of Ashton's La Fille mal Gardée, London. The Robert Joffrey Ballet is founded, USA.

1962 Nureyev joins The Royal Ballet. Australian Ballet is founded.

La Fille mal Gardée

1964 Civil Rights Bill passed, USA. Martin Luther King receives the Nobel Peace Prize.

1965 Flemming Flindt becomes Director of the Royal Danish Ballet. First performance of Kenneth MacMillan's Romeo and Juliet, London.

1968 First performance of Yuri Grigorovich's Spartacus, Moscow.

1969 First performance of Cranko's Taming of the Shrew, Stuttgart. Scottish Ballet is based in Glasgow. Darcey Bussell is born. American astronauts Neil Armstrong and Buzz Aldrin become the first men to walk on the Moon, and defy gravity.

1971 Dance Theatre of Harlem makes its professional debut in New York.

1974 Kirov dancer Mikhail Baryshnikov defects to the West and joins American Ballet Theatre. First performance of Kenneth MacMillan's Elite Syncopations, London.

1983 Nureyev becomes Director of the Paris Opéra Ballet. Peter Martins and Jerome Robbins become co-Directors of New York City Ballet. Peter Schaufuss becomes Director of Festival Ballet.

1986 Anthony Dowell becomes Director of The Royal Ballet.

1989 Berlin Wall comes down.

1990 Bolshoi star Irek Mukhamedov joins The Royal Ballet. Sadler's Wells Royal Ballet becomes Birmingham Royal Ballet. Festival Ballet becomes English National Ballet.

1991 Death of Fonteyn. Break-up of Soviet Union.

1993 Death of Nureyev.

1995 A balletomane buys a pair of Nureyev's ballet shoes at auction for £12,075. Modern dance choreographer Twyla Tharp makes her first ballet for The Royal Ballet.

Glossary

abstract ballets Ballets with no story or dramatic theme – dance for its own sake.

adage *ad-ahge* Slow and sustained steps and movements which flow from one to another.

alignment Relationship of one part of the body to another.

allegro *al-leg-row* Fast and lively steps which may include jumps and travelling steps. There is grand (large) and petit (small) allegro.

arabesque *arab-esk* The dancer balances on one leg with the other stretched and raised behind.

attitude *at-ee-tood* Rather like an arabesque except that the lifted leg is bent at the knee in a curve behind the body, instead of being straight.

arabesque

auditorium Part of the theatre where the audience sits.

backcloth Painted cloth which hangs down at the back of the stage as part of the scenery.

ballet de cour Court ballet of the 17th century with sumptuous costumes, music, dance, mime and processions.

ballet master Takes rehearsals, and sometimes organizes their schedule.

ballet mistress Takes rehearsals, and is usually responsible for rehearsing the female corps de ballet.

ballon Style of jumping in a particular 'bouncy' way, so that the dancer seems to hover in the air.

barre Wooden rail, fixed to the walls of a dance studio. Dancers use it to balance as they practise basic exercises.

baton Small thin stick used by the conductor to direct the orchestra.

battements frappés *bat-mon frap-ay* A barre exercise in which the foot is first flexed and then strikes against the floor, like a match against a box.

battements tendues *bat-mon ton-doo* A barre exercise in which the foot is stretched along the floor until it points.

batterie *battery* Steps where the legs are beaten together, such as an entrechat. There is petite (small) batterie and grande (large) batterie.

Benesh notation System of recording dance steps, invented by Joan and Rudolf Benesh in 1955.

changement *shonge-mon* A small jump which begins in fifth position with one foot in front and ends in fifth position with the other foot in front. Used as a basis for learning entrechats.

character dancing Traditional folk choreographed for ballets – an example is the Polish mazurka in Coppélia.

character role A part in a ballet which involves acting and mime rather than dance – two examples are the Queen in Swan Lake and Carabosse in The Sleeping Beauty.

choreographer Has the idea for the ballet and then arranges the steps and patterns so that they make a whole work of art.

classical ballet Style of dance based on rules laid down over centuries by French, Russian, Danish and Italian teachers and schools.

Classical ballets Usually Russian story ballets of the late 19th century which follow a particular pattern – such as Swan Lake and The Sleeping Beauty.

contemporary dance A 20th-century dance style which has different rules from ballet. For example, there is no pointe-work, feet can flex instead of point, and ribs and hips have different, less rigid alignments.

corps de ballet *core de ballay* Dancers who perform together as a group and do not dance solos or leading roles.

coryphée *corry-fay* Junior soloist, somewhere between the corps de ballet and soloist rank.

demi-caractère Dancing, or a dancer, with a comic or folk dance flavour, often technically gifted. Examples are Puck in The Dream and Alain in La Fille mal Gardée.

divertissement *dee-ver-tiss-mon* A display of dancing which is not central to the story of a ballet – such as the solos Dawn and Prayer in Act II of Coppélia, and Puss-in-Boots and the other wedding dances in Act III of The Sleeping Beauty.

divertissement

electro-acoustic Music made by electronic instruments such as synthesizers and samplers – used in some modern ballets.

en avant *on av-on* Forwards, as in fifth en avant, where the arms are held in front or forwards.

enchaînement *on-shane-mon* A series of steps linked together, like words making a sentence.

demi-caractère

en croix *on krwa* In the shape of a cross, as in a barre exercise when the movement is made forwards, to the side, to the back, and to the side again.

en derrière *on derry-air* Backwards, the opposite of en avant.

en diagonale *on dee-ag-on-ahl* Dancing that goes diagonally from corner to corner of a studio or stage.

entrechat six *on-tre-sha sees* A jump from fifth position in which straight legs cross over each other three times.

finale The end of a ballet, or in a Gala programme the climax to a series of divertissements.

flat A piece of painted scenery which stands upright at the side of the stage.

folk dance Dance of people all around the world as a part of everyday life. It is passed down through the generations and does not use a choreographer or complicated staging.

folk dance

fouetté *fwet-ay* A turn in which the working leg seems to whip in a circular movement, away from the supporting leg – like a spoon in a bowl of cake mix. Odile performs a series of 32 fouettés in Act III of Swan Lake.

grand allegro *grond allegro* Large jumping and travelling steps.

grands battements *gron bat-mon* A barre exercise in which the leg sweeps up to waist height or higher and is lowered in a more controlled way. Usually practised en croix.

grand jeté *gron shet-ay* A large travelling jump, with legs and arms outstretched.

grand jeté

jazz dance Began in the USA around 1917 and developed alongside jazz music. Based on African dance movements, jazz dance is used in ballets by Jerome Robbins and other choreographers.

Labanotation System of recording dance steps and ordinary movement, developed by Rudolf von Laban.

leotard Close-fitting costume, like a swimsuit, with or without sleeves, worn for ballet classes.

line The graceful curves and shapes made by a dancer's body in the space around them.

lyricism A way of dancing which is particularly graceful and flowing.

leotard

motif (or leitmotif) A phrase of movement or music, or an idea. It is repeated throughout a ballet, either to help tell the story or to make a pattern the audience can recognize. Examples are Giselle, where each character has their own music, and La Fille mal Gardée, where ribbons are used in many different ways throughout the ballet.

neo-classical Sometimes used to describe ballets developed by George Balanchine, based on Marius Petipa's classical ballets of the late 19th century.

notator Records the steps and movements of a ballet using Laban or Benesh notation.

pas de deux *pah deh deh* A dance for two people in ballet, usually male and female. Can be called a duet if they are of the same sex.

petit allegro *petty allegro* Small jumping and travelling steps performed in enchaînements.

physiotherapist Treats injured dancers. He or she has specialist knowledge of sports and dance injuries.

pirouette en dedans *piroo-ette on deh-don.* A step in which a dancer turns inwards, towards the supporting leg. Pirouettes are performed en pointe or demi-pointe.

pirouette en dehors *piroo-ette on day-or* A step in which a dancer turns outwards, away from the supporting leg.

plié *plee-ay* A basic ballet movement in which the knees bend.

pointe-work Dancing on the tips of the toes, en pointe, using specially hardened shoes. Performed only by women, except to give a special effect in a demi-caractère role, such as Bottom when he is a donkey in Frederick Ashton's The Dream.

en pointe

port de bras *por deh brah* The movement of the arms in ballet.

premier danseur Principal male dancer in a ballet company.

présage lift A lift in pas de deux, in which the male dancer holds the female high above him with his arms straight.

prima ballerina Principal female dancer in a ballet company.

promenade *prom-en-ahd* Sometimes part of pas de deux. The male dancer walks round the female, supporting her while she is en pointe in an arabesque or in an attitude.

repertoire The collection of ballets that are performed by a company. Students will be expected to learn some of the repertoire as part of their training. Sometimes known as repertory.

répétiteur Teaches the repertoire and takes rehearsals with the company. Usually a former dancer.

révérence Formal bow made by dancers at the end of a class or a performance.

Romantic ballets Ballets that are part of the Romantic movement in the early 19th century. They are usually mysterious fairy stories.

révérence

rosin Yellow crystallized chunks of distilled turpentine (a natural resin from trees) which are crushed to a white sticky powder. Used on ballet shoes to stop dancers slipping on the stage. Kept on a flat tray in the studio or the wings.

score

score The complete set of music or dance notation for a ballet.

social dance Dance for pleasure such as ballroom and disco.

solo A dance for one person.

special effects Sound and light used to create atmosphere such as thunder, mist and snow. Includes lasers, slide and video projections, and dry ice.

spotting Used by dancers to avoid becoming giddy while turning. Your eyes fix on one spot and try to return to the spot as quickly as possible.

technique Means two things. First, the features that are important to classical ballet, such as the steps, turn-out, pointe-work. Second, the skill with which a dancer performs these.

tempo The speed at which music is played by the orchestra.

temps de poisson *tom deh pwasson* A leap in which the body curves in the air, like a fish jumping out of water.

theme ballets Ballets that have no story as such but are clearly about something. Examples are MacMillan's Gloria, about the horror of World War I, and Ashton's Les Patineurs, about ice skating.

turn-out The way the dancer's leg turns out from the hip socket. Central to ballet technique.

tutu The ballerina's skirt made of many layers of gathered net, which can be very short (Classical) or calf-length (Romantic).

understudy Person learning a role who can stand in for another dancer. Also known as cover or second cast.

variation A dancer's solo, sometimes part of a pas de deux, sometimes part of divertissements.

virtuoso A performer or performance of brilliant technical skill.

Index

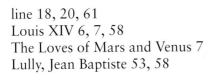

Acknowledgements

The publishers would like to thank the following
illustrators for their contribution to this book:

Victor Ambrus (Virgil Pomfret Agency) 22–23, 32–33;
Julian Baker 56–57; **Peter Dennis** (Linda Rogers Associates)
36–37; **Francesca D'Ottavi** 34–35; **Susan Field** 46–49;
Terry Gabbey (Associated Freelance Artists Ltd) 28*c/bl*, 29*tl/bl*,
30*tr/c/br*, 31*bl/tr*; **Pamela Goodchild** (B L Kearley Ltd) 9*tl*, 19*br*,
21*br*, 41*c*, 42*bl*, 43*tr/bl*, 50–51; **Adam and Christa Hook**
(Linden Artists) 24–25; **Christian Hook** 31*bl*, 40–41; **Biz Hull**
(Artist Partners) 12–13, 13*br*, 14*bl*, 14–15, 15*tr/cr*, 16*tr*, 16–17*c*,
17*t*, 18*br*, 20*tr*; **John James** (Temple Rogers Artists Agency)
38–39; **Nicki Palin** 6–7; **Helen Parsley** (John Martin Artists) 8,
9*br*, 44–45; **Clive Spong** (Linden Artists) 4–5; **Jean Paul Tibbles**
(Central Illustration Agency) 10–11, 20*b*, 42*r*; **Shirley Tourret**
(B L Kearley Ltd) 9*cr*, 14*r*, 15*b*, 17*r*, 18*t/bl*, 19*t/cr*, 21*t/bl*,
27*t*, 29*br*, 31*br*, 36*l*, 37*tl/r*, 43*br*.
Border ribbon and Sleeping Beauty miniatures by **Ian Beck**.

The publishers would also like to thank the following
for supplying photographs for this book:

Ancient Art and Architecture 7; **Catherine Ashmore** *endpapers*;
Bridgeman Art Library 8, 25, 51; **Bill Cooper** 21; **Anthony
Crickmay** 5, 19; **e t archive** 28, 30; **Mary Evans Picture Library**
26*t*; **Novosti Photo Library** 31; **Society for Co-operation in
Russian and Soviet Studies** 26*b*;
Tate Gallery 13; **Reg Wilson** 11;

and **The Benesh Institute, Anthony Crickmay, English National
Ballet, Robbie Jack, London City Ballet, The Metropolitan
Opera, The Royal Ballet** and **Scottish Ballet** for
their kind assistance.

The publishers gratefully acknowledge permission to reproduce
the following copyright material:

page 10, from **The Magic of Dance** by Margot Fonteyn © 1979
Fountain Productions Ltd, by permission of the author's estate;
page 34, from **Nureyev – an autobiography with pictures** © 1962
Opera Mundi, by permission of Hodder Headline plc.